Preface

When the Soviet Union launched the first space satellite, Sputnik 1, on October 4, 1957, it marked the beginning of the space age. Since then, space travel has developed rapidly. Man has landed on the Moon, put manned space stations into orbit, and launched space probes that send us pictures of faraway planets.

The general public has shown particular interest in manned space flights – the Moon landings, the record-breaking flights by Russian cosmonauts on board the Salyut and Mir stations, and the pioneering achievements of astronauts working on board the American Space Shuttle. The Russians and the Americans have also involved astronauts from other countries in their projects – the Space Shuttle carried out some of its most demanding and scientifically rewarding missions with the European-built Spacelab in its cargo bay.

The experience gained from these successful manned space ventures is now helping to shape the new International Space Station. The United States, Russia, Canada, Japan, Brazil, and the countries of the European Space Agency are working together to build this station, which will be much larger than any previous space station. The partners are contributing special technical skills, organizational experience, and scientific knowledge to help realize the project.

The construction and operation of the International Space Station will provide important technological benefits and many new ideas and economic possibilities for all countries involved. It will also help improve understanding between peoples of the world, since it brings many countries together in a huge project requiring the highest levels of cooperation and communication. It will also serve as inspiration to young people interested in careers in space travel.

Wolfgang Engelhardt

PUBLISHERS: Tessloff Publishing, Quadrillion Media LLC

EDITOR: Alan Swensen

PICTURE SOURCES:

Boeing Defense & Space Group: p. 25. Daimler Benz Aerospace: pp. 17, 61. dpa: p. 5. Wolfgang Engelhardt/Astro Verlag: pp. 4, 5, 6, 7 (NASA), 8 (NASA), 9, 10, 11, 12 (NASA), 13 (NASA), 14 (NASA), 15 (NASA), 18, 19 (NASA), 23, 24, 26, 27, 29, 30/31 (NASA), 32 (NASA), 33 (NASA), 34 (NASA), 35 (NASA), 37, 38 (NASA), 39, 40 (NASA), 41, 42, 43, 45, 49 (NASA), 50, 52, 53 (NASA), 54, 55 (NASA), 58 (NASA), 59 (NASA), 60, 62. ESA: pp. 16, 47. Lockheed: pp. 56, 63. McDonnell Douglas: pp. 44, 48. mps/Verlagsbereich Luft und Raumfahrt: pp. 7, 8.

ILLUSTRATIONS: David Ducros/ESA: pp. 2, 20/21, 28, 46, 51, 57, 64. Weigand: p. 36.

COVER: David Ducros/ESA

Translated by Ulrike Seeberger

Library of Congress Cataloging-in-Publication Data is available.

ISBN 1-58185-004-2

Printed in Belgium

Printing 10 9 8 7 6 5 4 3 2 1

Contents

The Idea of a Station in Space

When did people get the idea of building a space station? **4**

What did Wernher von Braun's proposed space station look like? **5**

Skylab — the First U. S. Space Station

How did the American Skylab Project start? **6**

What happened during the three Skylab missions? **7**

What results did the Skylab program yield? **8**

The Russian Salyut and Mir space stations

What was the significance of the American-Soviet ASTP-flight? **10**

How did the Salyut space station program get started? **11**

What were the successes of Salyut stations 6 and 7? **12**

What has the Soviet space station program accomplished? **13**

What do Western astronauts learn during stays on board Mir? **14**

Planning the International Space Station

What role did Space Shuttle labs play in the development of ISS? **16**

What kinds of experiments were carried out on Shuttle labs? **17**

Why is it so important to have a manned space station? **18**

Why were so many changes made during the planning stages? **19**

When were the Russians invited to participate? **19**

The International Space Station

What will the International Space Station look like? **22**

What components will be included in the space station? **24**

In what order will the ISS be assembled? **24**

What types of rockets will be needed to assemble the space station? **26**

How will supplies be delivered to the space station? **27**

The Costs and Benefits of the ISS

What will it cost to build and operate the International Space Station? **32**

Why are some interest groups opposed to the space station? **35**

Research On Board the International Space Station

What are the advantages of doing experiments on the ISS? **36**

What medical experiments will be carried out on the space station? **38**

What materials science experiments are planned for the space station? **40**

How will Earth sciences profit from the International Space Station? **42**

What kind of astronomical observations will be possible? **43**

International Contributions to the Space Station

What is the USA contributing? **44**

What does the American Crew Return Vehicle look like? **46**

What does Russia's contribution include? **47**

What is Japan's contribution to the space station? **49**

What will the European module include? **51**

What is the Canadian robotic arm like? **53**

Life and Work on the Space Station

What will an astronaut's life on the station be like? **56**

What will the Habitation Module look like? **58**

How will the experiment racks be used? **60**

Will there be hotels in space? **62**

List of Acronyms **64**

The Idea of a Station in Space

The wheel-shaped space station proposed by von Braun in 1952 (left) had a diameter of 225 feet. One of the chief advantages of his design was its modular construction. Scientists and engineers would build the space station elements on Earth and astronauts would then assemble them in orbit.

ACCORDING TO THE IDEAS developed by von Braun and his team of engineers, their wheel-shaped station would rotate slowly, creating a centrifugal force in the ring that would imitate the effect of gravity. It would have been about one third of the gravitational force on Earth. This would help eliminate the negative effects of weightlessness on the human body. We now know from experience that astronauts on long-term flights often have trouble dealing with weightlessness. His team calculated that the space station's atmosphere would need to be renewed every day with about 230 pounds of oxygen. Wernher von Braun also planned a drying system that would condense the water vapor released into the air through breathing and thus renew precious water resources.

When did people get the idea of building a space station?

The idea for a manned space station goes back to a time before space travel was even technically possible. In 1869 Edward Everett Hale published a story titled "The Brick Moon." In it he described a man-made station in orbit around the Earth. In 1923 the German-Rumanian rocket scientist Hermann Oberth included a sketch for a space station in his book "A Rocket into Interplanetary Space." The first detailed proposal came in 1928 from a German scientist, Hermann Noordung. His plans weren't simply imaginative – he provided detailed blueprints. In the 1950's German-American rocket scientist Wernher von Braun (1912-1977) planned a space station, basing his design on sound physics, and providing more complete drawings than any of the earlier attempts. He provided details for building the station elements, transporting them into space, assembling them in orbit, and for keeping the station supplied once it was operational. Von Braun had worked out the precise load-bearing capacity the rockets would need in order to ship the elements of the station into orbit and to deliver the supplies needed for continuous operation.

Wernher von Braun's plans were a big step towards realizing a manned space station in orbit.

WERNHER VON BRAUN'S bold technical vision also anticipated the "Hubble Space Telescope." He suggested placing a space telescope in orbit with a mirror 7.5 feet in diameter. Using a transport rocket, something like today's Space Shuttle, astronauts would fly to the telescope and service it. As von Braun imagined it, the astronauts would use a small "space taxi" to get from their transport rocket to the space telescope where they would change film cassettes and do repair work.

This was due not only to his engineering genius but also to his public relations skills. In a series of articles in "Colliers Magazine" he presented his plans to millions of readers. It was the first time the general public had seen plans for a space station. Realistic illustrations helped people visualize his proposed space station. The articles also discussed space travel, satellites, and Moon landings.

For a long time von Braun's proposal was the most realistic starting point for future plans. His studies convinced many that a rotating wheel was the best shape for a space station. As the wheel rotated around its axis, it would create a kind of gravity that would make it easier for the crews to tolerate long stays in space. The modular structure of the station was also practical. It would be relatively easy for rockets to transport the 20 modules into

What did Wernher von Braun's proposed space station look like?

Wernher von Braun

orbit and astronauts would assemble them there.

In his plans, von Braun took into account the limited carrying capacity of the rocket types conceivable at the time. They could only carry relatively small loads. To make the modules lighter, von Braun planned to use mostly synthetic materials. After the pieces arrived in space, workers would link them together to form a large tubular ring. The interior was divided into working and living spaces.

Along with the space station, von Braun planned a space telescope much like today's "Hubble Space Telescope." He also planned a large-format camera that would take pictures of the Earth at regular intervals. Astronauts wearing thick protective suits would go outside the station to service these instruments and change the film cassettes.

An artist's conception of astronauts doing maintenance work on von Braun's telescope.

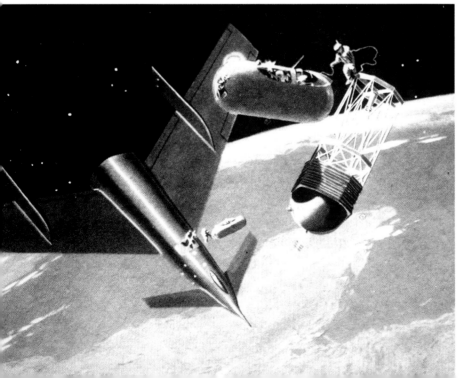

Skylab — the First U. S. Space Station

How did the American Skylab Project start?

Skylab was the direct successor of the Apollo Moon Program. By 1972, after six Moon landings, the American public had begun to lose interest in flights to the Moon. Many people thought these landings were a waste of money and protested against continuing the program. The government reacted quickly and cancelled the three flights still scheduled.

This meant that NASA suddenly had several large Saturn rockets and space capsules "left over" and could use them in a new program to study the Earth and the nearer regions of space. This is how the Skylab program came about.

Skylab was used for experiments in the fields of medicine, materials science, Earth observation, and astronomy — particularly solar research. Three teams of three astronauts stayed in the Skylab station — the first team for one month, the second for two, and the third for almost three months. During their stays they did pioneering work for space travel.

The space station proper consisted of the modified third stage of the large Saturn 5 carrier rocket. The rocket's hydrogen tank was converted into the astronauts' living and working quarters. It was approximately 22 feet in diameter and 50 feet long. Most of the station's operating systems and many of the scientific instruments were contained in this rocket stage. Special cupboards and refrigerators held the extensive supplies needed for the crews.

A powerful life support system supplied an atmosphere of 28 per cent oxygen and 72 per cent nitrogen with an air pressure of 0.3 bar. This is about one third of the air pressure on Earth. There was also a system for regulating the station's bearing in space. Sensors helped keep the station properly oriented and balanced.

THE SKYLAB ASTRONAUTS brought back from their missions numerous photographs showing the orbiting station in various positions against the backdrop of the Earth. The large solar cell panels always point towards the Sun for maximum energy yield. The huge parasol sunshield can be clearly seen above Skylab's main body. It kept temperatures inside the station bearable after the loss of the heat shield. The Skylab space station was launched on May 14, 1973, and orbited the Earth 35,000 times over a period of six years, until July 11, 1979, when it dropped into the Earth's atmosphere and burned up.

Skylab was almost luxurious compared to the first American space capsules. The astronauts could even take one shower per week, as demonstrated by Charles Conrad in the picture at right. The small tube-like shower cabin had to be sealed off completely, and the water was sucked out immediately. Otherwise there would have been water everywhere in the cabin due to the absence of gravity.

Some Skylab astronauts suffered badly from space sickness at the beginning of their missions. The typical complaints — headaches and nausea — usually went away after a few days.

One interesting experiment involved two garden spiders that managed to weave their fine webs on board the station in spite of the absence of gravity. They displayed amazing powers of adaptation to space conditions.

The above picture shows a close-up of the garden spider Arabella who "took part" in the Skylab 3 project.

On May 14, 1973 Skylab was launched from Kennedy Space Center in Florida on a two-stage version of the Saturn 5 rocket. Skylab weighed nearly 90 tons. It was placed in an orbit 270 miles above the Earth, with an inclination of 50 degrees toward the Equator, and an orbital period of 93 minutes.

What happened during the three Skylab missions?

It soon became clear that the heat and meteorite shield around the central section of Skylab and one of the large solar panels had been torn off during the rocket's ascent through the Earth's atmosphere. The second large solar panel was stuck and wouldn't unfold. This meant the station was without energy. For the moment, however, the protective shield that had been torn off was the main danger, since the inside of the station soon became dangerously hot.

On May 25, 1973, NASA launched a smaller Saturn 1B rocket that carried the first team of astronauts to the orbiting Skylab station in an Apollo capsule. Soon after docking, two astronauts climbed out of the capsule for a daring space walk. They were supposed to raise a temporary sunshield over the space station's central section. After several hours of hard work, they successfully completed the task. They had to wait four days, however, before the interior of the station was cool enough that they could leave the cramped capsule and enter the station. They then began their extensive research program.

Once they freed the remaining solar panel they had 16.7 kilowatts of electricity available — including power from the solar telescope. This was enough for most of the scheduled experiments. Thanks to the courage of the crew, the Skylab project was saved.

STATION had an overall size of 21 x 21 x 108 feet and included the large orbital workshop as well as a coupling adapter for docking with Apollo capsules and an air lock module leading to the main lab. The solar telescope was mounted separately and had its own cross-shaped solar array that was 81 feet across. A further solar panel, jutting out from the station's main body, provided energy to the station.

Left: Portraits of the nine Skylab astronauts. The space station is shown in the center.

Below: Paul Weitz at the telescope's operation panel.

> **What results did the Skylab program yield?**

On February 4, 1974 the three astronauts of the third Skylab team returned to Earth after 84 days and 1,260 orbits. With them they brought an extensive collection of magnetic tapes, exposed films, and materials they had tested. This third and last trip concluded the extremely successful Skylab project.

For a total of 170 days, this first space station had served as living and working space for three astronauts at a time — for a total of 513 man-days in orbit around the Earth. The crewmembers spent approximately 42 man-hours outside the station making repairs and changing the film in the solar telescopes.

All told, the Skylab yielded 183,000 photographs of the Sun and 40,000 of the Earth, and 63 miles of magnetic tape containing radar data from the surface of our planet. In addition, there were numerous astronomical photographs of large areas of the heavens. It would be difficult to count all the biomedical experiments and materials science tests the astronauts carried out in their weightless environment.

Unfortunately, NASA never put the second Skylab station into orbit, even though it had already been constructed. Instead of continuing the Skylab program, they concentrated on developing the Space Shuttle in the years that followed.

The experience gained during the Skylab project is now turning

THE **SKYLAB** ASTRONAUTS took films and photographs of the Sun, the central star of our solar system. They used the solar telescope in all ranges of the spectrum and were able to monitor these images immediately on a screen. Astronomers on Earth were also directly involved in the solar observations and connected up via special data links.

Soon after their arrival at Skylab, astronauts Charles Conrad and Joseph Kerwin left the safety of the space capsule. In a dramatic outboard maneuver, they managed to free the large solar panel that had become jammed.

THE SKYLAB ASTRONAUTS had to perform numerous repairs on the inside and outside of the space station to make it safe to live inside the station. After these initial problems were solved, the astronauts' work outside the station mainly involved servicing the gyroscopes in the altitude control system (the system regulating the station's orientation in space). These components caused a lot of trouble and had to be replaced several times. The life support system and the altitude control system also needed intensive maintenance.

in medical and technical fields.

Most of all, NASA's planners have realized the importance of well-trained astronauts for a large-scale space enterprise like this. Without highly skilled crews the entire Skylab project would have failed at the start. The courageous ventures outside the spacecraft saved the program. No mechanical apparatus could have responded to the crises that marked the start of Skylab as effectively out to be invaluable as the United States prepares for the much larger and more long-term "International Space Station" (ISS). The Skylab missions demonstrated how valuable an independent manned station is for scientific experiments as the astronauts did. The same is true for the many other repairs that became necessary in the course of the enterprise – not to mention the numerous successful experiments the astronauts carried out on Skylab.

The Three American Skylab Missions

	SL-1	SL-2	SL-3	SL-4
LAUNCH DATE	May 14, 1973	May 25, 1973	July 28, 1973	Nov. 16, 1973
ROCKET TYPE	Saturn 5	Saturn 1B	Saturn 1B	Saturn 1B
ORBITAL DATA	Height: 270 miles Inclination: 50° Period: 93 min			
CREW		Conrad, Weitz, Kerwin	Bean, Garriott, Lousma	Carr, Gibson, Pogue
FLIGHT DURATION	6 years *	28 days	59,5 days	84 days
NO. OF ORBITS	35,500	419	859	1,260
RESEARCH TIME		16,3 days	50 days	65 days
EVAs		3 (6.3 hours)	3 (14 hours)	4 (22.25 hours)
LANDING DATE*	July 11, 1979	June 22, 1973	Sept. 25, 1973	Feb. 8, 1974

* SL-1: burn-up   * for Skylab itself

The Russian Salyut and Mir space stations

An American Apollo capsule and a Soviet Soyuz capsule in a joint flight.

Another precursor of the huge International Space Station was the joint Apollo Soyuz Test Project (ASTP). It was started in mid-1975 by the American and Russian space agencies. In the course of this venture, an American Apollo capsule and a Soviet Soyuz capsule docked in orbit. The astronauts and cosmonauts (as Russian astronauts are called) were then able to visit each other's spacecraft.

For the ASTP project, each country had to allow the other partner extensive insight into their manned space projects. Each crew had to learn the language of the other crew so they could communicate during the docking maneuvers and during their joint work.

> **What was the significance of the American-Soviet ASTP-flight?**

Thanks to careful preparations, the joint flight went off without a hitch — almost. On July 15, 1975 the Soviet Soyuz 19 capsule lifted off from the Baikonur Cosmodrome, and the Apollo capsule started from Florida. They entered into an orbit at a height of 140 miles, 52 degrees inclination toward the Equator, and an orbiting time of 89 minutes. The two spacecraft docked on July 17, marking the start of a four-day combination flight of their crews.

Although most specialists agree that the Apollo Soyuz project was not very important from a technical or scientific standpoint, it did have a positive effect on the political relations between the USA and the Soviet Union. At that time the two countries — the major Western and Eastern powers — were still engaged in the "Cold War."

ONE OF THE TECHNICAL PREREQUISITES for a successful American-Soviet Soyuz-Apollo flight was a special coupling adapter. This allowed the two capsules to be connected in spite of technological differences. NASA built the complicated mechanism and launched it into orbit together with the three astronauts in the Apollo capsule.

THE AMERICAN ASTRONAUTS for the ASTP were Thomas P. Stafford, Donald K. Slayton and Vance D. Brand. The Soviet crew consisted of cosmonauts Alexei Leonov and Valeri Kubasov. Each team learned the language of the other team so they could communicate without difficulty.

THE FIRST SALYUT STATIONS had many problems, and Soviet politicians involved with the space program in these years demonstrated great patience. Finally, however, the Salyut program began to produce the technical and scientific results they had hoped for. The first space stations had only one coupling adapter on the bow. Later a stern hatch was added where supply capsules could dock. Now the Mir station, which was launched in 1986, is equipped with a multiple adapter making it possible for five capsules or modules to dock at the same time.

How did the Salyut space station program get started?

In the late 1960's the Soviet Union also began a major program aimed at landing a man on the Moon – just like the United States. After the fourth failure of the N1 rocket they developed for this program, they dropped the project. The Soviet government then shifted the focus of its manned space program in a more Earth-oriented direction.

This was the beginning of the Salyut and Mir space station programs. This shift was similar to the one in the United States, except that NASA had actually succeeded in landing several crews of astronauts on the Moon. After this unparalleled achievement NASA turned its attention to Skylab.

The American Skylab project

powerful system for monitoring and adjusting the station's bearings. It keeps the station in the right position relative to the Earth and the Sun. It also regularly lifts the station's orbit. This keeps the station from slowing down and dropping into the Earth's atmosphere where it would burn up.

Over the years the life support system used in the Soviet space stations has proved to be very reliable. Even under difficult conditions it maintains a breathable oxygen-nitrogen atmosphere with moderate temperatures and comfortable humidity levels.

A weak point in the Soviet space stations is their inadequate energy supply. This is partly responsible for another problem: the ineffective communication systems, i.e. radio and data transmission. Whenever the space station

Both Salyut 7 — shown here in the final stages of assembly — and the core module of the Russian Mir station consisted of several aluminum segments mounted one behind the other.

was abandoned after only three crews had visited the station, however. The Soviets, on the other hand, have put a total of seven space stations into orbit since 1971. Because of many technical problems the early Salyut models had very short life spans.

In the meantime, Soviet space stations have developed some important systems. They have a

was on the far side of the globe from Moscow, crews could only contact Moscow through relay stations on ships. In the early years of the Salyut program there were very few ships underway around the globe. Later on, relay satellites became available – but only on an irregular basis. Even today Russian Mir crews don't always have radio contact with ground command.

The real break-through in the Soviet Union's manned space program came with the Salyut 6 space station, which the Soviets launched in 1977. This model worked well over a period of several years. In the course of its operation it was occupied by many crews of cosmonauts. They were able to live and work on board the station for several weeks or months at a time.

What were the successes of Salyut stations 6 and 7?

For such long stays to be possible, the Soviets had to supply provisions for the station and its crews on a regular basis. During this phase of their space station program, the Soviet Union developed a sophisticated supply system using unmanned "Progress" capsules. These capsules can carry up to 2 tons of fuel, water, gases for air supply, scientific equipment, food, and other everyday items for life in a space station. They also bring mail and newspapers for the crews.

The Russians needed a new supply craft approximately every three months to keep the Salyut stations running smoothly. The same is true today for the Mir station. It wasn't until the Americans, Europeans, and Japanese started planning their own supply transport for the International Space Station, that they began to appreciate the accomplishments of the Soviet space engineers in this field over the past decades.

The Mir station, launched in 1986, was fitted with a multiple coupling adapter. This makes it possible for five spacecraft to dock at the same time. In the meantime four large expansion modules have been attached to Mir, making it into a very large space station.

The individual modules serve specific research fields such as materials testing, bio-medical research, Earth observation, and astronomy. Each module has its own solar panels and generates additional power for the operation of its instruments.

What has the Soviet space station program accomplished?

THE RUSSIAN SALYUT AND MIR SPACE STATIONS are powered by several large solar panels. Because of their low efficiency they manage to supply only a few kilowatts of electrical power. Although this is enough to ensure normal operation of the space complex, it doesn't leave much spare power for energy-intensive experiments.

THE RUSSIAN MIR STATION is a rather bizarre looking object with its many modules and wing-like panels (right). It consists of a central unit with a multiple coupling adapter at which four large expansion modules later docked, forming a cross-shaped assembly. The independent modules serve specific areas of research — for example materials testing, Earth observation, and astronomy. Each module carries its own solar cells for generating energy. The entire Mir station has an overall power yield of about 3 kilowatts. When the station is on the night side of the Earth, batteries supply energy for life support systems and for scientific experiments. The batteries recharge while the station is on the day side of its orbit.

All told, the Soviets — and now the Russians — have achieved some astonishing technical and organizational successes in the decades since their space station program was founded. The United States and the other nations involved in the International Space Station program hope to profit from this accumulated experience in the future. In particular, some of the cosmonauts from the Salyut 7 station and the more recent Mir stations have set remarkable records for long-term habitation in space.

The experiences of these cosmonauts show that, from a medical viewpoint, astronauts could certainly cope with the 2 to 3-year journey to Mars. To prevent their bodies from growing weak in weightless conditions — without gravity's resistance the muscles don't have to work as hard — men and women in space need to exercise regularly. They would need to be in top condition for a landing on the Red Planet and for the subsequent exploration.

The scientific achievements of the Soviet space station program are difficult to assess, however. This is primarily because detailed results of the Salyut and Mir experiments rarely appeared in scientific journals. For decades Moscow kept repeating the official formulas about successful experiments carried out on the space stations but didn't give any details.

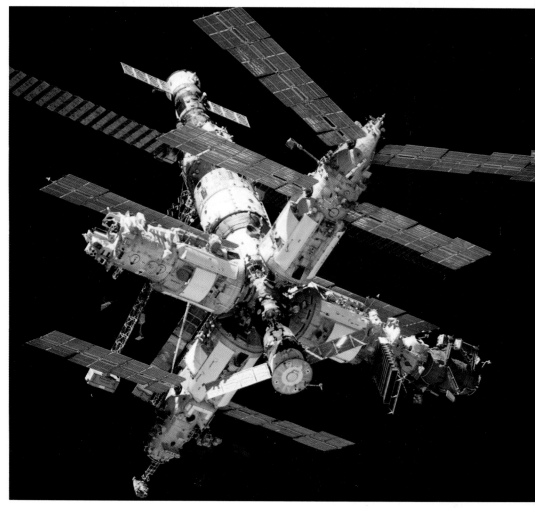

The Mir complex now plays an important role in preparations for the International Space Station. Especially since the political shift in the former Soviet Union, Western states are lining up to have their own astronauts participate in space flights and experiments on the Mir station. The French began participating in this special type of East-West cooperation even before the political shift took place. Astronauts from other countries soon followed – from Britain, Japan, the United States, and Germany, for example.

What do Western astronauts learn during stays on board Mir?

The United States has been granted the most intensive participation in the Mir space station. In preparation for cooperative work on the ISS, the United States Space Shuttle has docked nine times with the orbiting Mir complex. Each time the Shuttle and the Mir space station exchanged astronauts and large quantities of supplies and materials.

In the course of these cooperative exchanges, the two major space nations – who will also play the biggest role in the development of the International Space Station – have had an opportunity to test procedures they will need when assembling and operating the ISS. They have gained practice in important orbit maneuvers and docking techniques and also carried out joint research projects in orbit. All of this will later be part of the routine operation of the International Space Station.

MIR was launched in early 1986. It was the first to be fitted with a multiple coupling adapter at the rear. In the following years the Russians connected four large expansion modules for scientific research. They are dedicated to experiments in bio-medicine, materials science in conditions of weightlessness, as well as to the observation of the Earth and to astronomy.

Astronaut Mark C. Lee tests the new Simplified Aid for EVA Rescue (SAFER). The forward cargo bay is reflected in Lee's helmet visor in this 35mm exposure, taken through the aft flight deck windows of the Space Shuttle Discovery.

Space Shuttle astronauts have taken stunning photos of the orbiting Mir space station.

THERE ARE VERY FEW PUBLICATIONS reporting the results of Russian experiments carried out in microgravity. The reason for this is probably the long period during which Russian scientists had little access to related work carried out in the West. Another obstacle might have been the numerous technical hitches that plagued the early Russian space stations. They left the cosmonauts precious little time for scientific experiments.

Data on the Russian Salyut/Mir space stations

Station	Launch	Visits	Remarks	End
Salyut 1	Apr 19, 1971	Soyuz 10+11	first Russian space station	Oct 11, 1971
Salyut 2	Apr 3, 1973	no visits	first military space station	May 22, 1973
Salyut 3	Jun 24, 1974	Soyuz 14+15	also for military use	Aug 24, 1975
Salyut 4	Dec 26, 1974	Soyuz 17+18B	only non-military use	Feb 2, 1977
Salyut 5	Jun 22, 1976	Soyuz 21-24	last military space station	Aug 8, 1977
Salyut 6	Sep 29, 1977	Soyuz 25-40	first station of the 2nd generation	Jul 29, 1982
Salyut 7	Apr 19, 1982	Soyuz T5-15	last Salyut station	Feb 7, 1991
Mir 1	Feb 20, 1986	Soyuz T15-TM27	first station of the 3rd generation	Still in space

Planning the International Space Station

What role did Space Shuttle labs play in the development of ISS?

Another important step toward the development of the International Space Station were the space laboratories built by NASA and the European Space Agency (ESA). They were not independently orbiting stations, but rather modules that were fitted into the cargo bay of the Space Shuttle and used during its flights. NASA built the U. S.

The Space Shuttle supplies energy for the labs and provides radio communication with ground command. Specially trained scientist-astronauts carry out experiments around the clock. Spacelab divided its crews into a "blue" and a "red" team and each team worked in 12-hour shifts.

These labs have given astronauts valuable experience working on experiments in microgravity, but they are far from ideal. The preparation time for a Spacelab

FROM A SCIENTIFIC AND TECHNICAL POINT OF VIEW, some of Space Shuttle's most ambitious and productive flights were those that carried the European-made Spacelab in its hold. The main emphasis was on biomedical research on the effects of microgravity on the human body.

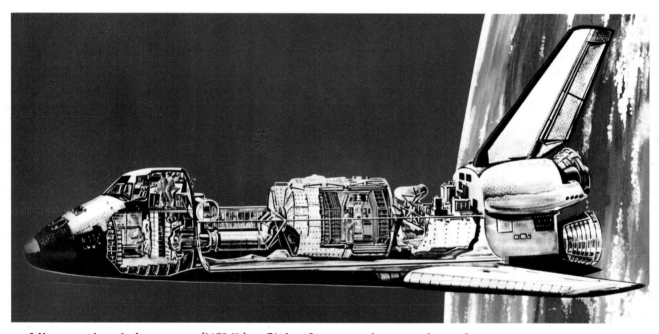

Microgravity Laboratory (USML) and ESA built "Spacelab." There is also a commercially financed laboratory called "Spacehab" that flew with the Shuttle. These labs were technical and scientific research stations designed for use in space. Numerous astronauts have worked in them, carrying out hundreds of biomedical and technical experiments in microgravity.

flight, for example, was about five years. Around 5,000 technicians and scientists were involved in the process. The total cost for each flight was nearly 600 million dollars. Because of this, the Spacelab mission in 1998 will probably be the last one. In the future, microgravity experiments will be carried out on the International Space Station now being assembled.

The European-built Spacelab is an 18-foot-long cylindrical capsule, 12 feet in diameter. On either side of the central aisle are experiment racks. The life support system is located under the floor. During its missions, Spacelab is firmly anchored in the hold of the Space Shuttle. Astronauts move back and forth between the cockpit and Spacelab through a short tunnel.

The first Spacelab mission commissioned by ESA took place in autumn 1983 as part of the ninth Space Shuttle flight. Among the crew was the German physicist Ulf Merbold (right), a payload expert. He was the first non-American on board a Space Shuttle.

THE EUROPEAN SPACE-LAB is the immediate precursor of the lab modules on the International Space Station. In the course of a dozen or so Shuttle flights, astronauts developed the technical procedures and above all the scientific guidelines for all the experiments that will soon be performed on board the ISS. The United States has also used the Spacelab on several missions. Most of the research missions have been international enterprises, however, so that several nations could share the enormous costs for each flight. Specially trained payload experts are in charge of the biomedical and materials science experiments. They work around the clock, in two shifts.

What kinds of experiments were carried out on Shuttle labs?

The Shuttle lab experiments attempted to discover how materials, processes, and human beings or other organisms perform in weightlessness — or microgravity, as scientists call it. The astronauts themselves were the object of some of the experiments. These experiments investigated the causes and effects of space sickness. About half of all astronauts suffer from this during the first days of a flight. The symptoms are nausea, vomiting, and headaches — similar to the symptoms of seasickness.

Scientists can't predict prior to the flight which men and women will suffer from this particular "adaptation problem" — as NASA somewhat euphemistically calls it — during long-term weightlessness. This disorder is probably caused by a disruption of the body's sense of balance, which at first has trouble functioning properly in microgravity. In most cases the symptoms disappear after a few days. There are, however, people who are unable to regain their sense of balance under conditions of weightlessness.

Medical experiments on these labs also investigated a number of other effects of weightlessness on the human organism. Examples of such effects are the rush of blood to the upper body and to the face, muscle atrophy (mainly in the legs), loss of calcium in the bones, and a decrease in the red blood cell count.

Such effects could prove to be a serious obstacle to manned space flights to more distant planets, flights that would take several years. An idea shared by many earlier space station theorists such as Wernher von Braun might offer a solution. He proposed building a ring-shaped space station that would rotate around a central axis, like a wheel. The centrifugal force created by the spinning motion would give the astronauts at least a limited degree of gravity.

One of the drawbacks of all labs on Space Shuttle is that their use is limited to the brief duration of the Space Shuttle flights — they can only stay in space a little over two weeks. After that the Shuttle's supplies are exhausted. The scientists would gladly continue their research projects, but the space glider has to return to Earth after sixteen days at the latest.

As exciting as it is, scientific space flight is not an adventure playground for scientists. It is an important tool that can help us gain a better understanding of our world. In the end, its real purpose is to improve living conditions on Earth. The International Space Station will be a major research institution in orbit. Its scientists will examine the biological functions of humans and other

life-forms under conditions of weightlessness, study the physics and chemistry of specific processes, observe the Earth's surface, and explore the universe.

In addition to its technical and scientific uses, the space station project will also have some indirect benefits. The world's major industrial nations have agreed to cooperate on the ISS. This is a sub-

stantial step in strengthening international cooperation and promoting global economic growth and world peace. The ISS will join the Apollo Moon landings as a milestone in the history of human achievements.

In 1984 President Ronald Reagan proposed building a major space station. He later invited other Western nations to cooperate in this project. Canada, Japan, and the countries of the European Space Agency accepted his offer. In 1988 the space agencies of

these countries signed an official agreement. It established a long-term partnership with mutual responsibilities and rights in the building and operation of the future space station. It also specified each member's share in the station's cost and in the use of research facilities, as far as this was possible at this early date. They named the project "Freedom."

SINCE 1984 NASA has been examining various space station concepts. One of these was the "Freedom" design, which had a single horizontal grid structure as supporting element (left). Two American modules and one European and one Japanese module were to be connected to this structure at the center. Two large solar arrays on the left and right were to supply the station's energy.

AS DESIGN CONCEPTS CHANGED — and they did so every few years — NASA also made regular updates of its cost estimates. As the size of the station shrunk, however, the costs did not go down. Instead the project became more and more expensive. In keeping up with the frequent modifications, NASA spent a billion dollars on computer studies alone. Some critics say that this large sum of money might have paid for a small space station in orbit.

An artist's rendition of the Space Shuttle approaching the "Freedom" Space Station.

ONE OF THE CONDITIONS Russia set before agreeing to participate was that America agree to increase the space station's orbital inclination from 28 degrees to 51.6 degrees. This allows the Russians to launch their cargoes directly from the Baikonur Cosmodrome near Tyuratam in Kazakhstan without having to decrease the capacity of their carrier rockets. The ISS orbit now runs relatively far to the north and south, however, and this is a disadvantage for the Space Shuttle, which is launched closer to the Equator — in Florida.

Soon after President Reagan made the pioneering proposal, NASA submitted a preliminary design for the space station. Since then the plans have been modified and adapted several times.

> **Why were so many changes made during the planning stages?**

At first, NASA experts envisioned a so-called "one keel" shape with a single central truss structure. Computer simulations showed that this construction was too unstable, however.

Then, for a while, the so-called "dual keel" model was the trend. It consisted of a rectangular truss structure roughly the size of a soccer field. This framework supported four lab modules that were attached inside the rectangle. The plans called for two gigantic solar arrays on the sides that would supply the station with energy. This design was soon scrapped as well, however, because it had turned out too large, too complex, and too expensive.

While designers continued to rework the plans and make new proposals every year or two, NASA kept updating the cost estimates. As the size of the station shrunk, however, the cost did not fall, but instead kept on rising.

The greatest changes in the space station's design came about after the political situation in the Soviet Union changed. Now it seemed like a good idea to invite the Russians to participate in the project. In late 1993, President Bill Clinton invited Russia to join the ISS project, and the Russian government accepted.

> **When were the Russians invited to participate?**

This meant that all the technical, organizational, and financial aspects of the space station project had to be reconsidered. All of the participating countries — the USA, Europe, Japan, and Canada — agreed that Russian involvement was both necessary and desirable. On the one hand, it would help integrate Russia more fully into the community of nations. On the other hand, the Russians collected a wealth of experience with their Salyut and Mir stations. This experience will be very valuable to the ISS project.

The Spacelab D-2 mission organized by the Federal Republic of Germany and carried out in the spring of 1993 was a major success. The crew included, from left: Mission Specialist 1 and Payload Commander Jerry L. Ross, Mission Specialist 2 Bernard A. Harris Jr., and German Payload Specialists Ulrich Walter and Hans Schlegel. During one of the many special events televised during the Columbia's flight, crewmembers used German and American flags as a backdrop in the science module.

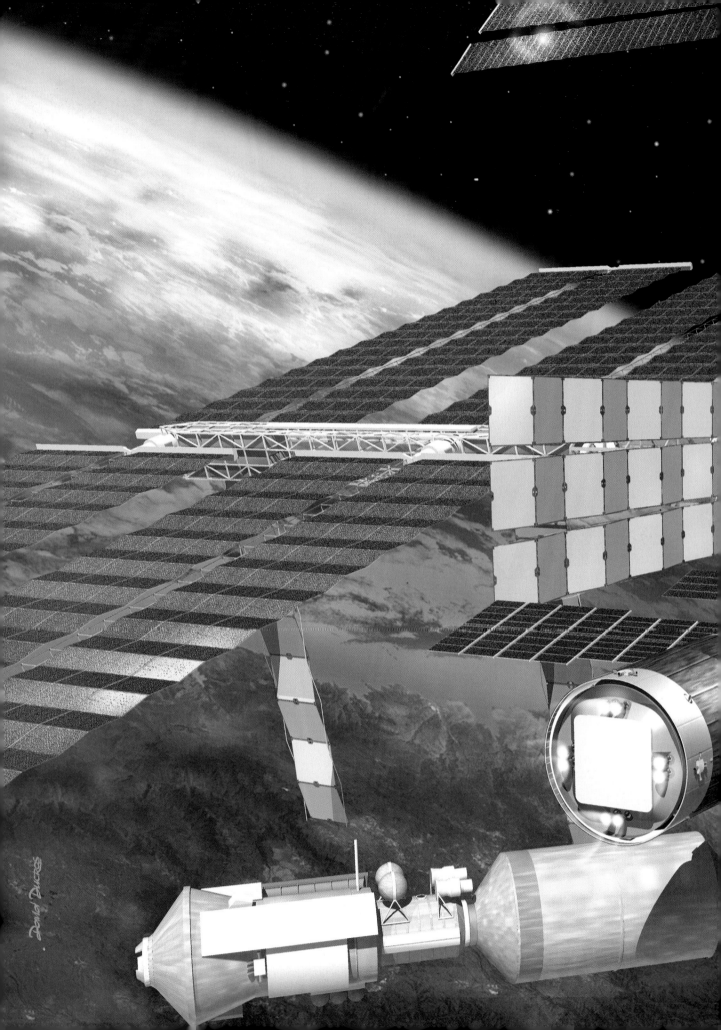

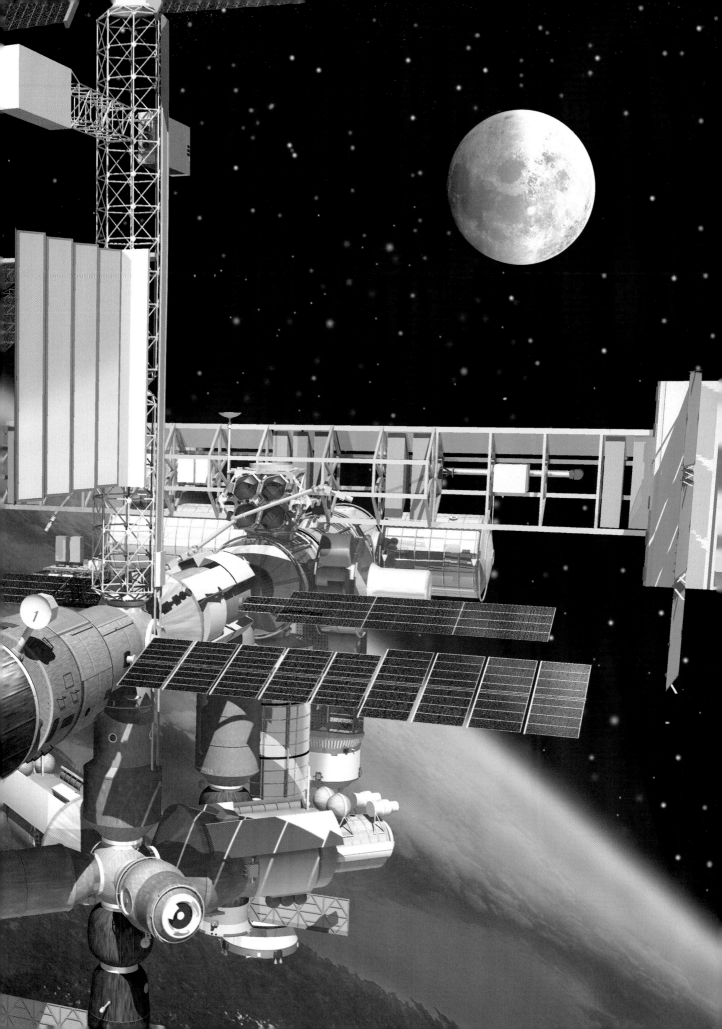

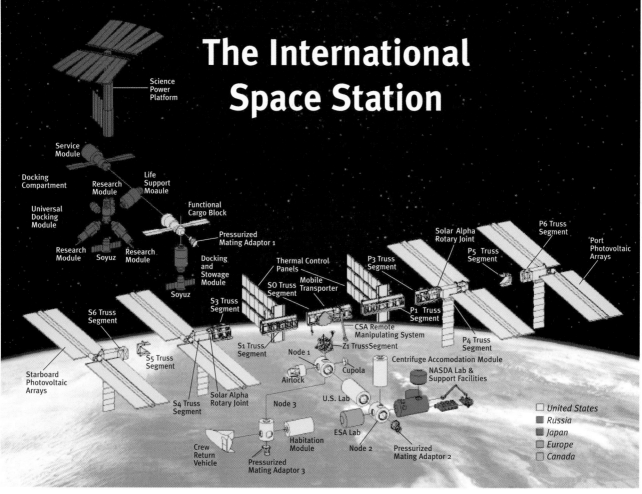

The International Space Station

Science Power Platform

Service Module

Docking Compartment

Research Module

Life Support Module

Universal Docking Module

Functional Cargo Block

Research Module

Soyuz

Research Module

Pressurized Mating Adaptor 1

Docking and Stowage Module

Soyuz

Thermal Control Panels

Mobile Transporter

SO Truss Segment

S3 Truss Segment

S6 Truss Segment

S1 Truss Segment

S5 Truss Segment

CSA Remote Manipulating System

Z1 Truss Segment

Node 1

Cupola

Airlock

Centrifuge Accomodation Module

NASDA Lab & Support Facilities

Starboard Photovoltaic Arrays

S4 Truss Segment

Solar Alpha Rotary Joint

Node 3

U.S. Lab

ESA Lab

Crew Return Vehicle

Pressurized Mating Adaptor 3

Habitation Module

Node 2

Pressurized Mating Adaptor 2

P3 Truss Segment

Solar Alpha Rotary Joint

P5 Truss Segment

P6 Truss Segment

Port Photovoltaic Arrays

P1 Truss Segment

P4 Truss Segment

☐ United States
■ Russia
■ Japan
☐ Europe
☐ Canada

The overall dimensions of the International Space Station will be 290 feet by 356 feet — larger than two football fields.

What will the International Space Station look like?

On Earth — with its gravity — it would weigh more than 500 tons. The largest element of the ISS is the central truss system with large solar panels at each end. They will be 356 feet long and positioned perpendicular to the station's flight path, like the wings of a plane. The cylindrical working and living modules will be located towards the center of the truss system.

The two large American modules — living and working quarters — will be attached at the center of the truss assembly. The large Japanese Experiment Module (JEM), with its logistics module and platform for outboard experiments, will be located on the port side (left), relative to the station's flight direction. The European laboratory COF (Columbus Orbital Facility) will be mounted on the starboard side (right). Two large radiators will also be attached to the central grid structure. They will radiate excess heat from the station out into space.

A node element connects the Japanese and the European modules to one of the American modules. This cylindrical connecting element is also fitted with a coupling dock for the American Space Shuttle as well as with a special air lock. The astronauts can leave the space station through this "door" to work on assembling the ISS — and then later on for experiments

This exploded diagram shows all the major lab modules and other technical systems that will make up the International Space Station. The elements will be transported into orbit and assembled there. The Russian ISS modules are on the left, the American and international modules on the right.

Toward the end of 1998, following the launch of the Russian Functional Cargo Block (FGB) and Service Module, the United States will send Node 1 — the central connecting unit between the American and Russian segments — and two adapters into orbit. This will enable the complex to function at a minimum capacity with living and working space for two to three astronauts. By mid-1999 this station core could possibly be available for first limited use. If construction proceeds as scheduled, the space station could begin routine operation with full experimental capacity in late 2004.

or for inspection and maintenance operations.

The central node element will connect the American Laboratory Module and the Russian Functional Cargo Block (FGB). This "block" is a spacecraft in its own right, complete with its own power supply, navigation, propulsion and communications systems.

Linked to the FGB is the Service Module. This module will serve as living, working, and sleeping quarters for three crewmembers. At the far end of the cylindrical Service Module there will be another coupling dock for unmanned supply transports such as the Russian supply rocket Progress.

Above the connecting element between the Service Module and

plex is assembled. The main solar panels will be attached at the ends of the central truss system. Together with the solar arrays on the Russian segment of the station, these panels will generate a total of 110 kilowatts of electricity. Almost half of this will be available for scientific experiments. Whenever the space station is on the night side of its orbit, batteries will supply power.

During the construction period, three astronauts will man the space station. Later, when it is operational, six or seven men and women will live on board the ISS. The Space Shuttle will exchange crews every three months. Astronauts will be chosen on the basis of qualifications and nationality.

The solar panels consisting of light-sensitive cells are glued onto a flexible backing and rolled up for transport into orbit. They will then be unrolled during assembly in space. The picture above shows one of the solar panels under construction.

the FGB a tall truss structure rises — the Science and Power Platform (SPP). It supports a second large solar array that will supply energy to the Russian station elements. The European claw arm will also be fastened to this tall grid tower. It will be used to lift the Russian station modules into position as the space station com-

The national quota is determined by each partner nation's share in the overall cost of the project.

The "International Space Station" (ISS) — as it is now officially called — will orbit the Earth once every 94 minutes at an altitude varying from 210 to 287 miles. Its orbit will lie in a plane inclined 51.6° from the Equator.

The International Space Station

What components will be included in the space station?

will consist of two dozen different construction elements. Each of these components is given an acronym for quick reference. The central truss structure, for example – the Integrated Truss Assembly – is called the ITA.

The orbiting space station will contain a total of seven pressur-ized modules with an overall lab volume of about 43,000 cubic feet of living and working space. All together, the American, Japanese, and European lab modules will accommodate 33 standardized laboratory racks. These racks will hold the experiments. According to the latest schedule, the construction of the ISS will begin in the fall of 1998 and should be finished by the beginning of 2004.

The International Space Station and the Space Shuttle, seen from above, with measurements.

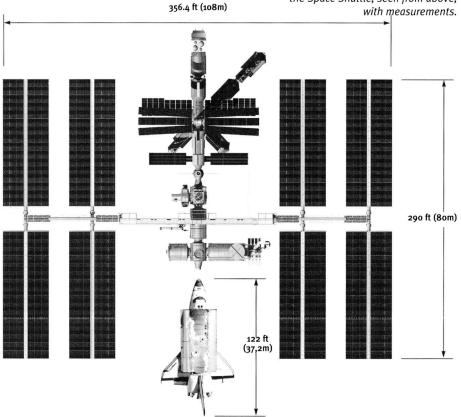

356.4 ft (108m)

290 ft (80m)

122 ft (37,2m)

ASSEMBLY OF THE INTERNATIONAL SPACE STATION in orbit will be a very difficult and risky undertaking. Planners cannot possibly predict all the dangers that might arise. According to NASA's calculations, the various teams of astronauts will have to perform a total of more than 1,000 hours of strenuous extravehicular work. Scientists and technicians have tested the necessary construction procedures in simulations on Earth. In large water tanks where the effect of gravity is nearly eliminated, the astronauts practice the construction techniques they must be able to perform.

ASTRONAUTS working outside the station will need to use spacesuits. A spacesuit is constructed like a small space capsule. It supplies the astronaut with oxygen, normal air pressure, and humidity. It also protects the astronaut from the extreme temperatures in outer space and contains a radio system for communication with crewmates on board the space station. An astronaut couldn't live outside the station without a spacesuit. While walking in space astronauts are secured by a steel tether attached to the station.

ISS construction was originally

In what order will the ISS be assembled?

scheduled to start in December of 1997. Financial and technical difficulties in Russia delayed the beginning of work by about one year, however.

The first element to be placed into the 220-mile-high orbit will be the 20-ton Functional Cargo Block (FGB), financed by the U. S. and built by the Russians. A Russian Proton rocket will carry it into orbit.

After this, the central node (Node 1) and the Russian Service Module (SM) will be mounted. In the summer of 1999, the first segment of the main truss (ITA) will be put into orbit. The central truss

THE INTERNATIONAL SPACE STATION will be assembled step by step. Two of the first elements launched into orbit will be the Russian FGB and the Service Module. The Russian research modules RM1 and RM2 and the Life Support Module (LSM) will be connected to the Universal Docking Module (UDM) near the end of the assembly. The UDM will also serve as the link between these later modules and the first two Russian modules.

consists of 12 separate segments. Solar arrays, radiators, and antennae will be connected to the central truss as it is completed. In late 1999 the large robotic arm — the Space Station Remote Manipulator System (SSRMS) is scheduled to be installed. It will play an important role in the assembly of the space station.

The American laboratory module (US LAB) is scheduled for launch in October of 1999. Between the years 2000 and 2002, the station's capacity will be expanded with the addition of the two Russian research modules (RM1 and RM2) and the Japanese

One of the American node elements during construction.

(JEM) lab module. The European lab (COF) will be added in 2003. The American Habitation Module (US HAB) will be connected in early 2004, and will be the last major element. This module will provide

room for four more astronauts. Six to seven people will then be permanently stationed in orbit. Routine operation and experimental use is scheduled to begin several months later, in the fall of 2004.

Before the station elements can be sent into orbit, however, they must first be dismantled into smaller pieces in order to fit through the Space Shuttle's cargo hatch — 13.5 feet by 48 feet — or into the Russian Proton rocket's cargo bay, which is even smaller. It takes a great deal of intelligence and skill to design the individual elements so that they still function properly after technicians dismantle them for transport and astronauts reassemble them in space.

It is crucially important that Russian and American space agencies adhere to all rocket and Shuttle launch dates for transporting the various ISS elements into orbit. This is not an easy task with such a gigantic technical project. Russia in particular has had to cope with many difficulties. The United States has begun working out plans for erecting the space station without the Russian contributions, or at least with only the Functional Cargo Block and the Service Module.

The completed ISS elements — the modules, the central truss structure and all additional equipment — will weigh over 500 tons. Once

> **What types of rockets will be needed to assemble the space station?**

they are finished and thoroughly tested they will be launched into orbit over a period of about five years. This is a major organizational challenge for the American and Russian space agencies. Following the current schedule, the assembly will require 43 launches — 4 Proton, 5 Soyuz, and 34 Space Shuttle flights. Each Space Shuttle can carry a cargo of about 20 tons. Many more flights will be required to transport crews and supplies during the assembly.

It wouldn't take anything as catastrophic as a Shuttle explosion to upset the schedule — technical problems have frequently made it necessary to postpone launching the Space Shuttle. The same is true for the Russian Proton and Soyuz rockets.

Such problems would naturally lead to major delays in the completion of the International Space Station. Any cargo lost in launch accidents will have to be rebuilt from spare parts — if there are any. Whatever happens, the partners in the space station project have several exciting and stressful years in store before the ISS is finally assembled and orbiting the Earth.

At least 20 Soyuz flights will lift the unmanned Progress transporter into space to bring fuel to the space station. This is needed for the propulsion system that regularly adjusts the ISS orbit. Without

THE AMERICAN SPACE SHUTTLE — seen at left, during lift-off — will play a key role in the construction of the International Space Station. With each launch it can carry one major element into orbit. The crew of the Shuttle will then help to install the part. From the rear control panel in the Shuttle's cockpit the astronauts can operate the Orbiter's robotic arm, lift the payload from the transport hatch, and place it in the proper position on the space station.

Between 1998 and 2004, the American Space Shuttle is scheduled to make 27 flights that will carry ISS elements into orbit. It will also bring a new astronaut crew each time and transport the previous one back to Earth. Of these 27 flights, 21 will carry ISS construction elements and 6 will transport equipment for the scientific experiments.

JAPAN, too, has long-term plans to employ its own H2A carrier rockets to deliver supplies for its module, the JEM. By the beginning of the next decade this new, stronger type of carrier rocket should be ready for use. Laws protecting the water and the fishing industry near Tanegashima Space Center strictly limit the number of launches, however. Japan is also planning to develop a transfer stage for its rocket. Like the ATV on the Ariane 5 rocket, it would be used to transfer cargo to the space station.

FROM A NUMERICAL STANDPOINT, Russia will carry the largest load for the construction of the ISS — 41 flights. The powerful Proton rocket (seen at right, during lift-off) will be particularly useful, since it is capable of carrying large, heavy modules and structures. Russia will also launch 10 Soyuz rockets, each of which will either propel a capsule with 3 astronauts or a Progress supply capsule into orbit.

ALL OF THE MAJOR SPACE STATION PARTNERS have long-term plans for developing their own rocket systems and integrating them into International Space Station operations. They will then be able to launch their own supplies and won't have to depend on other partners to provide costly transport services. This "mixed fleet" will also make operating the space station safer. In the long run, relying only on the Space Shuttle for supply and astronaut transport would be too risky.

such adjustments the station would gradually sink into the Earth's atmosphere.

Although Russian and American rockets will carry most of the cargoes, the European Ariane 5 rocket is scheduled to take one load of equipment to the space station.

Once the space station is completed, its routine operations will still be dependent on regular transport launches that can bring crewmembers and sufficient quantities of supplies to the station. As the Russian Salyut and Mir space stations have shown, this is the decisive factor in operating a space station successfully. If the ISS is to fulfill its goals, the Space Shuttle, the Soyuz rocket — whether carrying manned space capsules or unmanned Progress transporters — and the Proton rocket must all function reliably on a regular basis.

Other partners are also considering building their own manned space capsules in the near future. This would provide more possibilities for transporting crewmembers to and from the ISS.

Plans for keeping the ISS supplied make a distinction between supplies for individual countries and supplies for the station as a whole. The first group includes above all the transport of astronauts and consumer goods into orbit and back. It also includes provisions and spare parts for the country's experiments and their actual delivery to the space station under the supervision of the relevant ground control center.

How will supplies be delivered to the space station?

The individual countries will either produce and deliver their supplies independently or pay another partner for providing them.

The second group deals with the operation of the space station as a whole. It also includes the operation of the two central space station control centers, the Space Station Command Center (SS-CC) and the Payload Operations and Integrations Center (POIC) in the United States. All ISS partners will

Overview of the International Space Station, seen from above.

have to contribute their share of the cost of providing these services. Instead of making financial payments into the joint space station funds, partners are encouraged to contribute services and organizational support.

The partners could contribute their share by providing space transport services, by making communication networks available, or by assuming ground control oper-

ational costs. Europe, for example, plans to contribute its share by providing the transport services of its Ariane 5 rocket. This rocket can transport about 20 tons into orbit. According to early projections the European Space Agency will need to launch an Ariane rocket with an unmanned Automatic Transport Vehicle (ATV) every 18 months.

Project partners will be granted use of the ISS in proportion to their contribution to the infra-

structure and the service elements. Partners with their own lab modules, such as Japan with the Japanese Experiment Module, are automatically allocated 51% of their lab's capacity. NASA will be given 20% of each lab's capacity — compensating the U. S. space agency for its leading role in coordinating and maintaining the overall complex. The other partners who provide infrastructure elements for the space station will share the remaining 29%.

THE INTERNATIONAL SPACE STATION'S present form is a combination of earlier American and Russian designs. Integrating the new Eastern partner has created an entirely new set of conditions for all parties involved. It has influenced the technical design of the orbiting complex, the organization of the project, the scientific research program, and the share of the operating costs that each partner must assume.

THE SO-CALLED REBOOST MANEUVERS are an important element in the plans for ISS operations. They regularly "lift" the space station's orbit. Even at a height of 250 miles there are still remnants of the Earth's atmosphere and the resistance these remnants create — friction — gradually slows down the ISS, and as it slows, it begins to drop toward the Earth. To prevent it from dropping into the atmosphere it will regularly receive a "boost" from a transport rocket. For safety reasons, NASA has called for two independent systems that will perform this task: the Russian Progress capsule and the European ATV upper stage.

EXCITING AND STRENUOUS TASKS await the Space Shuttle astronauts within the next few years. They will be taking ISS elements into orbit and will help with the assembly of the space station complex. The large Canadian robotic arm (SSRMS) will be used in the course of these operations. It will lift the large structures from the Shuttle's load hatch and place them in the correct position in the complex. Astronauts will operate this Remote Manipulator System from the rear control panel on the flight deck of the Shuttle.

SOME CRITICS have suggested that manned space flights should be abandoned altogether. Instead they propose building a fully automated, unmanned space station. Past experience suggests, however, that a radical change such as this would only make the project more expensive. It takes specially trained personnel with highly developed analytical abilities and improvisational talents to keep a space station operating on a long-term basis and to carry out complex scientific experiments.

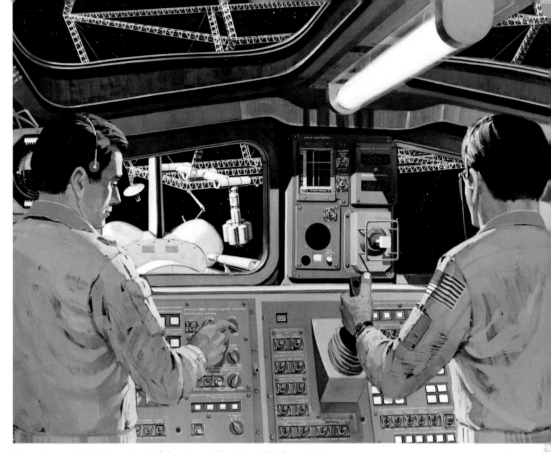

Two astronauts in the cockpit of the Space Shuttle guide the robotic arm.

Data on the International Space Station

Size	290 feet by 356.4 feet (79.9 by 108.6 meters)
Total weight	502.5 tons (1,005,021 lbs.)
Number of modules	7
Laboratory volume	1593 cubic yards
Orbiting altitude	210-280 miles
Orbital inclination	51.6 degrees to the Equator
Position deviation	maximum 5 degrees per axis
Degree of weightlessness	1 millionth of Earth gravity (10^{-6}g)
Uninterrupted time intervals for experiments	30 days
% of Earth's surface covered by ISS orbit	85%
Experimental capacity (excluding Russian modules)	33 international standard payload racks
External experiment platforms	538 square feet (50 m²)
Total power supply	110 kilowatts
Power available for experiments	46 kilowatts
Data transfer rate	
ISS to Earth	32 megabytes per second
Earth to ISS	72 kilobytes per second
Service intervals	4 flights per year
Crew size	1998–2003: 3; starting 2003: 6–7

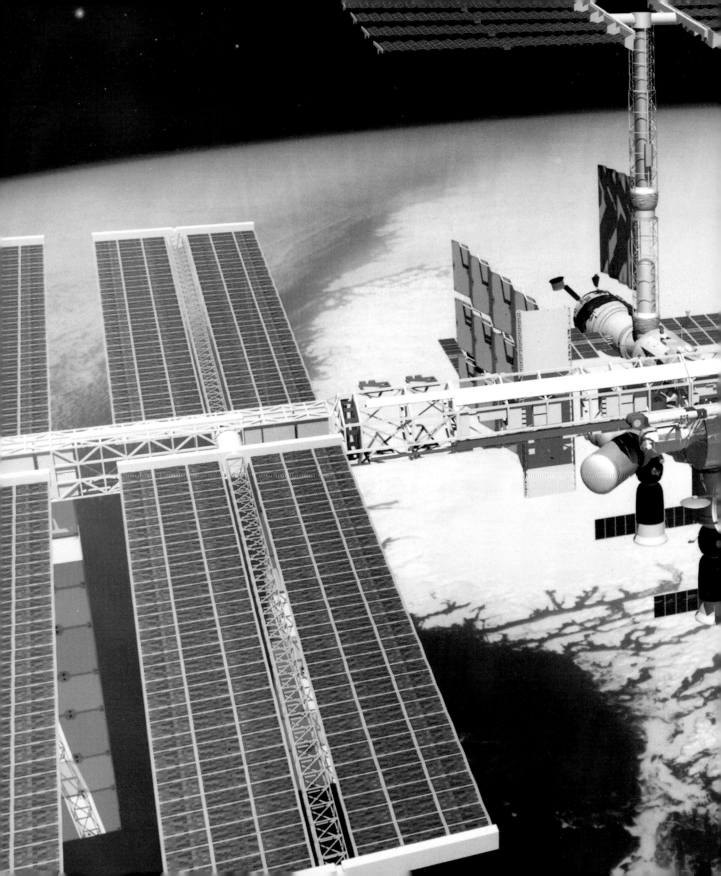

In order to introduce the International Space Station to the public through the media (magazines, TV, etc.) the American and European space agencies have commissioned a large number of impressive illustrations. This picture shows what the large complex with its branching modules and solar arrays will look like in orbit. In front you can see the smaller European COF-module and the longer JEM with its exposed platform for experiments. Each module shows the initials of its sponsor space agency — ESA in Europe and NASDA in Japan. The tower (SPP) bearing the smaller solar array is connected to the Russian station complex with its many modules.

When looking North during their flight over the Atlantic, the astronauts will be able to see the Southern tip of Greenland from a height of 240 miles — as in this artist's rendition.

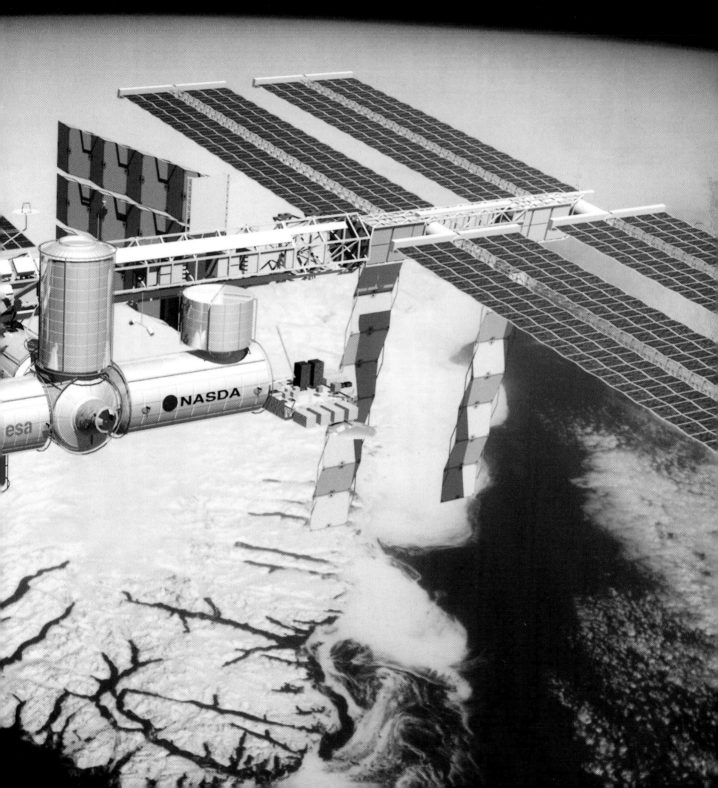

The Costs and Benefits of the ISS

What will it cost to build and operate the International Space Station?

As the major partner in the ISS project, the United States has also contributed the most support both in planning and in finances. NASA emphasizes the fact that the new space station is superior to the previous Freedom project in several respects. This is due in part to the experience the Russians have made available to the project. The new design also provides for larger lab facilities, more electrical power, a longer life span for the station, a larger crew, and better organization. It offers all of this and still costs 5 billion dollars less than the Freedom project would have cost.

According to current estimates, by the time the ISS is completed, it will have cost the Western ISS partners 60 billion dollars. The United States will contribute 12 billion dollars, and the other partners will pay 35 billion dollars. NASA estimates that an additional

THE USA AND RUSSIA are working together closely in their preparations for the International Space Station. The Space Shuttle has docked with the Mir station nine times. Each time, it carried a new American astronaut into orbit and delivered supplies and important spare parts for defective station systems.

The American Space Shuttle docking with the Mir space station.

THE SPACE STATION is also very important from a political point of view. It fosters international cooperation, as has already been demonstrated by the American Space Shuttle's flights to the Russian space station. The years of cooperation on the ISS project will also help nations and individuals to overcome political and cultural barriers. The photo on the right is a reminder of such possibilities. It was taken during a visit of the STS-81 American Shuttle team on board the Mir space station as guests of their Russian colleagues from the Soyuz TM22 team.

INTERNATIONAL GUEST ASTRONAUTS go through 1 to 2 years of preparations before they can participate on Mir flights. For this they go to Moscow and live in "Star City," where most of the training facilities are located and where their Russian colleagues also live. The biggest challenge for all candidates is learning the Russian language. After that, the would-be cosmonauts must familiarize themselves with the technical operation of the Soyuz transport capsules and the Mir station.

13 billion dollars will be needed for the first ten years of operation.

In absolute terms, these sums are enormous. They will be spent by the major space nations over a period of about 25 years, however. And these sums will not be meaninglessly "blasted" into space, as some critics claim. The money will create a huge number of jobs for technicians, engineers, scientists, and managers. Seen in this light, the space station becomes a major job creation program for all countries involved – in addition to the great scientific and technological benefits it will bring. A manned space station will also cost little more than an unmanned space project – as NASA has pointed out to politicians who are particularly critical of the project. So far Congress has allocated only $2.1 billion per year to NASA for the ISS. This is only 0.7% of the entire annual federal budget and less than 16% of the annual NASA budget.

United States participation in the International Space Station will cost each American taxpayer about 8 dollars per year. Studies carried out by American industry have shown that each dollar invested in space travel will return 2 dollars to the economy. The American aerospace industry in particular, with hundreds of thousands of jobs and an annual turnover of 33 billion dollars, will certainly benefit from the ISS.

Similar conditions apply in the other partner nations. The other countries spend a lot less money on the ISS than the United States does, however. German, French, and Italian taxpayers each pay less than one dollar annually towards the construction of the COF-Module and the other European contributions to the space station.

From the space station astronauts will be ideally situated to observe the interaction between "solar wind" — particles coming from the sun — and Earth's sphere of influence: its radiation belt, magnetic field, and atmosphere. One of the results of this interaction is the phenomenon we call the Polar Lights, which can be seen in higher latitudes. From the space station, scientists will be able to study more precisely the effects of long-term solar particle radiation and unfiltered ultra-violet light on astronauts and other organisms. The same is true for the study of micrometeorites. These are microscopic bits of cosmic dust that, over time, weaken or damage the surface of almost all materials in space — for example, the lenses of cameras and telescopes. Because of their high speed of impact — several miles per second — even the tiniest micrometeorites pose a considerable danger for the space station if they penetrate the aluminum body or one of the windows. If these holes weren't patched up immediately, the space station's atmosphere would leak out into the vacuum of space. During its many years in orbit, the Mir space station (below) has been hit several times by micrometeorites. They did not cause any serious damage, however.

THE NINE SPACE SHUTTLE FLIGHTS to the Mir station and the regular exchange of astronauts have prepared Russia and the United States well for their cooperation on the International Space Station. This picture was taken after the successful docking of Shuttle mission STS-89 from January 22nd to January 31st. Ten astronauts and cosmonauts form a human oval on board the Russian space station, demonstrating their freedom from gravity.

There are people who oppose manned space flight in general and the space station in particular. Some scientists oppose the project because they are afraid that the ISS project will drain financial resources away from research projects not directly connected to the space station's research programs.

> **Why are some interest groups opposed to the space station?**

Another criticism leveled at the ISS concerns the relatively modest results of previous space lab experiments — for example, experiments on the effects of weightlessness. Earlier space labs are not necessarily comparable, however. Previous research missions were simply too short to yield meaningful results in many fields of research. They were also too far apart — so far there has been about one Spacelab flight per year and it lasted a maximum of two weeks and focused on different issues and experiments each time. We don't have a clear picture of the results such experiments might yield over time. It might one day be possible to produce materials in microgravity that are superior to anything we can produce here on Earth — but it will take more extensive experiments to find out if this is possible or not.

Some also claim that manned flights could be done equally well by unmanned, automated vehicles. Supporters of the ISS point out that only human beings combine the training and creative intelligence needed to correct technical problems on the station or to evaluate unexpected lab results. There will be three "robotic arms" on the ISS to assist the astronauts, but there are as yet no robots with the combination of intelligence, adaptive skills, and dexterity that is characteristic of human beings.

Research On Board the International Space Station

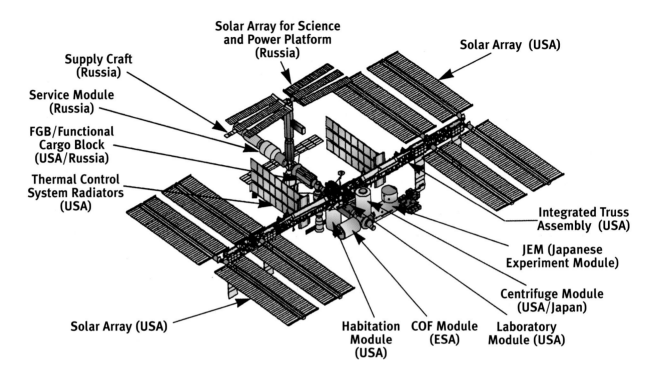

Solar Array for Science and Power Platform (Russia)

Solar Array (USA)

Supply Craft (Russia)

Service Module (Russia)

FGB/Functional Cargo Block (USA/Russia)

Thermal Control System Radiators (USA)

Integrated Truss Assembly (USA)

JEM (Japanese Experiment Module)

Centrifuge Module (USA/Japan)

Solar Array (USA)

Habitation Module (USA)

COF Module (ESA)

Laboratory Module (USA)

What are the advantages of doing experiments on the ISS?

Except in specially controlled laboratory conditions, the force of gravity influences everything that happens on Earth. Gravity often masks other forces that are at work in the chemical, physical, and biological processes that scientists study. On the ISS scientists will be able to investigate these processes in microgravity, free from gravity's obscuring effects. Technically speaking, microgravity is not actually the complete absence of gravity, however, but rather a very, very weak gravity — one millionth of the pull of Earth's gravity.

The value of microgravity for scientific experimentation cannot be overestimated. For example, gravity causes the heavier particles to settle out of a mixture and collect at the bottom of the container — a process called sedimentation. In microgravity these particles don't settle to the bottom but remain "suspended" in the mixture. Gravity also causes cooler masses of water or air to sink and warmer ones to rise — this movement is called convection. In microgravity there is no convection. As a result, flames don't rise into an elongated shape as they do on Earth, but rather have a rounded form. Results of experiments in microgravity may make it necessary for scientists to reformulate some of the laws of physics and chemistry.

Scientists are particularly interested in the effects of microgravity

THE SPACE STATION is an extremely complex technical structure in orbit. Its elements have to be carefully balanced to avoid any instability. The Western modules are easily distinguished from the Russian part of the ISS complex. The large solar panels will supply more than 100 kilowatts of electrical power for the orbiting station.

THE SPACE STATION will provide plenty of opportunities for complex long-term experiments. Researchers will have time to study slow processes like crystal growth.

on humans and on other living things — from single-cell bacteria to the most complex life forms.

The ISS will be better suited to these experiments than previous space stations were. The Shuttle flights that carry Spacelab are limited to about 2 weeks and there are long waits in between flights. Mir has less than a quarter of the lab space that the ISS will have, and much less energy for experiments. Scientists will now be able to perform uninterrupted, long-term experiments that would have been impossible before.

Research on scientific fundamentals will involve several different areas:

• Medical studies will look at the effects of weightlessness on circulation, on the immune system, on the muscular system, and on our sense of balance.

• Biological experiments will examine the effects of space radiation on sensitive organisms, and study the growth of plants in the absence of gravity.

• Materials research will investigate the formation of metal alloys, the growth of semiconductor crystals, and the behavior of materials at extremely high temperatures.

• Experiments in physical chemistry and fluid physics will look at the behavior of liquids and gases in weightlessness.

The benefits of the ISS won't come solely from the experiments, however. The technical, scientific, and organizational efforts needed to build the ISS will fuel significant advances in all nations involved —

just as the Apollo space program did in the USA 30 years ago.

Even in its developmental phase, the ISS is already a driving force in research and development. It has produced new, highly efficient heating and cooling systems, efficient water and air cleaning systems, and powerful waste disposal and recycling facilities.

Scientists are now preparing numerous medical experiments that will continue research begun on previous space labs. Most of these experiments will focus on the effects of microgravity on humans and on other plant and animal life.

What medical experiments will be carried out on the space station?

Gravity plays an important part in the growth and functioning of all living things on Earth. The sudden cessation of this natural constant has significant consequences for processes going on in these life forms. The effects of microgravity on humans during long-term space travel will be one focus of biomedical studies on the ISS. Much of the research, however, will be devoted to improving human health on Earth.

On Earth, the effects of gravity interfere with the growth of protein crystals and make it difficult to get precise data on the structure of these crystals. The higher quality of crystals grown in microgravity will provide researchers with more accurate data. This data will then be used in developing new drugs for the treatment of diseases such as AIDS. The growth of crystals takes time, and the continuous operation of the ISS will allow

MEDICAL EXPERIMENTS on board the Spacelab demanded great personal commitment. The astronauts had to take frequent saliva, urine, and blood samples. They also had to submit to strenuous lung tests, as German astronaut Hans Schlegel (below) is doing on the D2 mission.

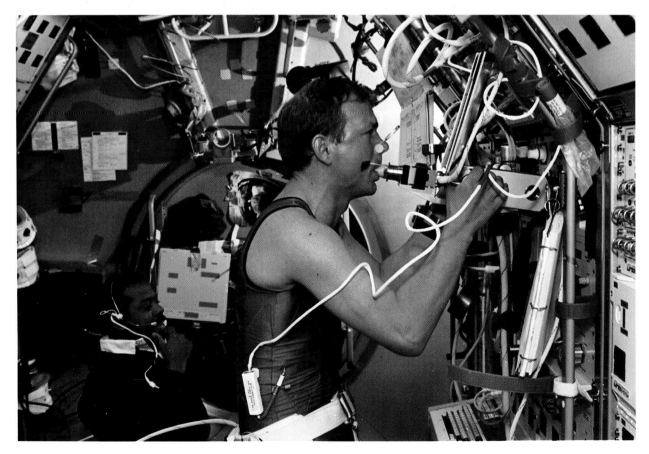

The illustration above shows astronauts assembling the Space Station. The robotic arm is clearly visible at the far right.

scientists to move forward much more quickly than was possible with Mir or Spacelab.

Because of sedimentation — the heavier elements sinking in a mixture — it is hard to grow cell cultures of human tissue in labs on Earth. The results are usually 2-dimensional rather than 3, as in the human body. In orbit such cultures grow more like tissues in the body do, producing 3-dimensional specimens that more accurately simulate tissues in the body. Such tissue cultures allow researchers to investigate cancer and other cellu-

lar diseases outside the body, with less risk to patients.

The study of plant growth in microgravity may lead to advances in biological research. We still don't know how a plant's roots grow downwards under the influence of gravity while its blossoms reach toward the Sun. In the near future the ISS will certainly provide opportunities to study the causes of gravity-related phenomena like this. This research could lead to the methods for cultivating agricultural plants with higher yields and greater resistance to diseases.

Materials science has been an

What materials science experiments are planned for the space station?

important part of space station research from the beginning. Materials science is the study of the structure, properties, and formation of materials — in other words, the study of a material's molecular structure; of its ability to resist heat, conduct electricity, withstand pressure, and so on; and of methods for producing the material. Materials science experiments have been a major part of the research on previous space stations and labs. To better understand the ways materials perform, scientists investigate basic phenomena like:

• cohesion (atoms, molecules, and ions sticking together due to electrical attraction)

• convection (currents in liquids or gases caused by differences in temperature and density)

• osmosis (movement of substances through porous membranes)

• adhesion (material sticking together due to molecular attraction)

• sedimentation (heavier elements settling out of a mixture)

The following are just a few examples of previous experiments on materials in microgravity:

• The fluid module developed by German scientists for Spacelab has been used to investigate the behavior of oil and water in orbit.

• Astronauts have performed interesting experiments on melting silicon and various metals. Scientists on Earth then examined the structure and properties of the samples they produced.

• Tests with small airplane turbine blades made of high-temperature resistant alloys produced impressive results. The astronauts on Spacelab heated the blades and

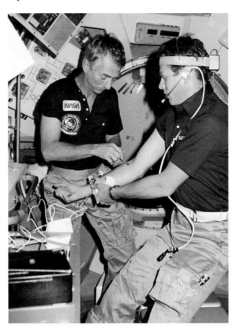

then cooled them down to alter their atomic structure and thus improve heat resistance.

• Experiments with silicon crystals show promising results. When grown in microgravity, the crystals developed a much finer structure. Such crystals would produce faster and more versatile computers.

• In addition, researchers in space developed metals with improved self-lubricating characteristics for sliding bearings in engines. They function with ten times less friction and thus increase the lifetime of the machine considerably.

• During one Spacelab mission, new aluminum casting methods for airplane and car chassis were tested. The units produced are much stronger and therefore much more durable.

• A further experiment in orbit looked at boiling processes. Scientists were looking for new ways to

SCIENTISTS are now planning numerous experiments that astronauts will carry out on the space station. Previous scientific research aboard Mir and the Space Shuttle has played an important role in selecting and designing the experiments.

Astronauts Dr. Owen Garriott (left) and Byron Lichtenberg perform medical experiments in Spacelab on Shuttle flight STS-9 in the fall of 1983. The headband Lichtenberg is wearing measures his brain waves and is connected to a recording device. He wore both devices during his waking hours throughout the mission as part of a study of space adaptation.

IN THE END, most of the research in microgravity will have tangible benefits for the people on Earth who finance the space station with their taxes. In cooperation with laboratories on Earth, the larger space station will determine which materials might be enhanced through processing in microgravity. Researchers have planned long-term experiments lasting weeks or months to investigate various fundamental laws of physics and chemistry — and perhaps even discover new ones.

improve the efficiency of steam generators for power stations.

• Researchers also tested the behavior of flames in microgravity. The findings may help design more efficient combustion engines for cars and jets, and new furnaces for low-exhaust, cost-effective power stations. An increase of 2% in airplane combustion efficiency would lead to fuel savings of $2 billion a year in the United States alone.

Even in these initial experiments we can see the possibilities for practical application in the future. This is why industry is now taking a closer look at the results, hoping to exploit them commercially some day. Most of these experiments will be repeated and expanded on the ISS. The advanced research facilities and uninterrupted research time on the ISS will make it possible to obtain even more precise results.

The commercial implications of such research are tremendous. For example, it may be possible to create new polymers (special synthetic materials) on the ISS that would have a wider variety of uses than present polymers, and enhanced properties. They could be used in the production of new paints, for example, or more comfortable contact lenses, faster computer chips, and superconductors that will make it possible to transfer electricity over long distances with virtually no loss in power.

View of the Space Station from above. The Space Shuttle, which regularly supplies the Station with provisions, has just docked at the docking bay.

EARTH OBSERVATION from the ISS could have many practical applications. Scientists will be able to follow cloud movement in the atmosphere and develop more accurate methods of predicting the weather. They will be able to monitor ozone in the atmosphere, particularly in the polar regions, and to carry out long-term observation of potential climatic changes on individual continents. By monitoring water flow from melting snows, they may be able to predict floods. It may even be possible to detect earthquakes, volcano eruptions, forest fires, landslides, and other natural disasters more quickly.

How will Earth sciences profit from the International Space Station?

In its orbit more than two hundred miles above the Earth's surface, the ISS will be an ideal platform for observing both our own planet and outer space. Here it will be free from the disruptive influence of Earth's atmosphere. Of course we already have satellites with sensitive cameras that serve a similar purpose, but they have to function automatically, without human assistance. The ISS will be equipped with the latest instruments for Earth and space observation, but more importantly, there will be scientists on board who can immediately evaluate results, make adjustments, and oversee and correct the functioning of the equipment.

The orbital track of the ISS will cover 85% of the Earth's surface, and this 85% of the Earth contains 95% of the planet's population. With its advanced cameras and instruments the ISS will be able to analyze and record cloud formation and movement, vegetation patterns, atmospheric quality, land use, and many other facets of our world. The information gathered may help us predict and prepare for major environmental events such as floods, severe cold or heat, and droughts.

SPECIAL INFRARED INSTRUMENTS will be able to monitor growing conditions throughout the world and perhaps even detect mineral deposits. From the space station's high altitude scientists will also be able to scan the vast ocean surfaces that play such an influential role in our weather, or track the depletion of rain forests in the tropical regions of South America, Africa, and Asia.

NEW RADAR SENSORS can monitor the Earth's surface even at night and in cloudy weather. The space station will be fitted with conventional optical cameras and electronic scanners as well as microwave antennae, and will be able to capture images of the Earth's surface at regular intervals around the clock.

What kind of astronomical observations will be possible?

Hubble Space Telescope has shown astronomers — both professional and amateur — that an observation point outside the Earth's atmosphere can collect remarkable astronomical data. The ISS will have its own facilities for space observation. They will not be as

flares or coronal mass emissions (the emission of highly charged plasma particles from the Sun) can be seen much better from a mobile space station outside the Earth's atmosphere than from stationary sites on Earth. The station can also monitor solar radiation blocked by the Earth's atmosphere.

Experiments will have to take into account the regular interruptions caused by the station's

Astronomical instruments on board the space station will be highly maneuverable and astronauts will be able to direct them easily toward new objects appearing in the sky — like the Hale-Bopp comet, pictured above.

powerful or specialized as some of the space satellites used for such purposes, but they will have the advantage of human operators who can respond quickly to unpredictable events as they occur. External platforms on the ISS will make viewing possible in virtually every direction. Astronauts will also be able to make repairs and adjustments on faulty instruments, change the film in cameras, and exchange electronic sensors whenever necessary.

The ISS is ideally suited for research in solar physics. It will regularly examine events on the Sun or in its atmosphere — the solar corona. Phenomena like solar

orbit – when it moves to the night side of the Earth every 45 minutes, for example, and no solar observations can be made. This dark phase is ideally suited for observing the remaining night sky, however. Without interference from the Sun's rays, scientists can see the dimmer objects in the far reaches of the universe more clearly.

To avoid blurring caused by astronauts' movements, observation of the Sun, the planets, and the stars will probably be scheduled for periods when the astronauts are sleeping. The telescopes can be programmed to move automatically to a specific region of the sky and to store the images received.

International Contributions to the Space Station

What is the USA contributing?

NASA will bear the largest share of the costs of building and operating the International Space Station—about 49%. In return, the United States will control a total of 23 payload racks either directly or by agreement with other partners. NASA has reserved 40% of this capacity for its own scientific experiments and commercial product development. The other 60% will be made available to the international scientific community, and research institutes can rent space for experiments.

The United States is contributing many hardware components to the ISS. The most important are:

- the American laboratory module (US LAB),
- the habitation module (US HAB),
- 4 large solar power arrays,
- 3 node elements, and
- the central truss (ITA or Integrated Truss Assembly)

The American lab module is 39 feet long and has room for twelve standardized payload racks, plus an "express rack" designed to permit quick installation of short-term experiments. The module is equipped with electrical, water, heating, and cooling systems powerful enough to run numerous experiments. US LAB will be the first laboratory installed on the ISS. It is scheduled to be placed in orbit in the fall of 1999.

Like US LAB, US HAB is also 39 feet in length and 15 feet in diameter. The module contains sleeping quarters for four astronauts, toilet, shower, and washroom, and a kitchen and eating space for the whole crew. There are also exercise facilities and leisure activities for the crew, and a small infirmary for emergency medical treatment.

The US LAB module will be attached to the middle of the central truss assembly, which is over 300 feet long and 13 feet across. The truss is the framework for the space station. The US HAB module will be attached to Node 1, the element connecting the US laboratory with the Russian-built FGB. At each end the truss will support the four large US-built solar arrays, each of which is composed of two large, 42-by-120-foot panels. The truss will also

THE FIRST AMERICAN NODE ELEMENT deployed — named "Unity Node" — will connect NASA's experimental and living modules to one another and to the Russian FGB module. The node also serves as a distribution station for vital supplies and as storage space for various materials for the astronauts. The large observation cupola pictured below affords the crew a spectacular view of their station, the rapidly moving surface of the Earth, and the stars.

foot rotor's rapid spin will approximate the effect of gravity. In this way biological and medical specimens can be subjected to precisely controlled doses of gravity after experiments in microgravity. In addition to the large centrifuge, the same module provides space for four standardized experiment racks.

The United States will also supply the life support system for the Western modules of the ISS. This system will maintain oxygen levels, humidity, and temperature in the pressurized areas. A constant temperature of about 68° Fahrenheit is important not only for the crew, but also for the sensitive scientific instruments. After all, the outer surface of the space station is exposed to direct sunlight and temperatures can rise as high as 212° F. The United States will also furnish the communications system that will provide for data interchange and radio contact with ground control. NASA is further responsible for the stabilizing system, which constantly monitors the orbiting station's orientation relative to the Earth and the Sun, and adjusts it as necessary. At regular intervals, the space station also needs to be lifted up to an orbiting altitude of 280 miles from the Earth. This will be performed at first by the Russian Progress capsule and later by the European ATV as well.

NEARLY ALL OF THE MAJOR AMERICAN ELEMENTS of the International Space Station are shown together in this illustration. The rigid truss assembly crosses the upper half of the picture. The U. S. laboratory module is attached to it in the middle of the truss, along with the Unity Node and its lookout cupola. The enclosed living quarters (US HAB) are mounted below the Unity Node. The nose cone of a docked Space Shuttle is visible in the background. The Space Shuttle will be the primary means of transportation between the space station and Earth for both astronauts and materials.

support a number of external platforms for experiments and the large Canadian robotic arm. This robotic arm will be an important tool for the astronauts as they assemble the parts in orbit.

The first two of the American node elements (Node 1 and Node 2) connect the individual lab modules. Supply lines in the nodes provide water, electricity, and oxygen to the various pressurized modules. Data communications also run through the nodes.

Japan has been commissioned by the USA to build a centrifuge module, which will simulate the conditions of Earth's gravity in the weightlessness of space. The centrifugal force produced by the ten-

Because a sojourn in space presents many dangers to the station's crew, plans for the ISS also include an escape vehicle.

What does the American Crew Return Vehicle look like?

This Crew Return Vehicle (CRV) is intended to bring the astronauts back to Earth in case of an emergency. In developing the CRV, NASA engineers drew on the agency's experiments in the 1960s with "lifting bodies," small, winged space vehicles that re-entered the Earth's atmosphere from orbit and landed in controlled flight. These experimental vehicles were equipped with a life-support system, heat shielding, limited maneuverability, and a large, steerable parachute. Small skids softened the landing on solid ground. The Crew Return Vehicle will be something like one of these "lifting bodies."

In preparation for the final CRV project, scientists and technicians are now developing a small experimental vehicle, the X-38. In March 1998, an aircraft carried the first test model to an altitude of 23,000 feet and released it in order to test its low-speed flight characteristics. Numerous other tests like this will follow before an X-38 first performs an actual landing maneuver from orbit in the year 2000.

The Crew Return Vehicle will be about 30 feet long and have stubby wings with a 15-foot span. It will weigh some five and a half tons, and be transported into orbit by the Space Shuttle. The CRV will consist of a cabin that can accommodate six astronauts and a propulsion section with a rocket engine to slow the CRV during re-entry into the atmosphere. It will also carry an orientation system, a radio, and emergency equipment.

The CRV is scheduled to be ready for operation by 2003. Until then, Russian Soyuz capsules will be docked at the space station to return astronauts to Earth in case of emergency.

NASA has chosen what it calls the "lifting body" shape — a small, maneuverable space glider with landing gear and short wings — for its Crew Return Vehicle (CRV). As the picture below shows, the shape looks something like a beluga whale.

46

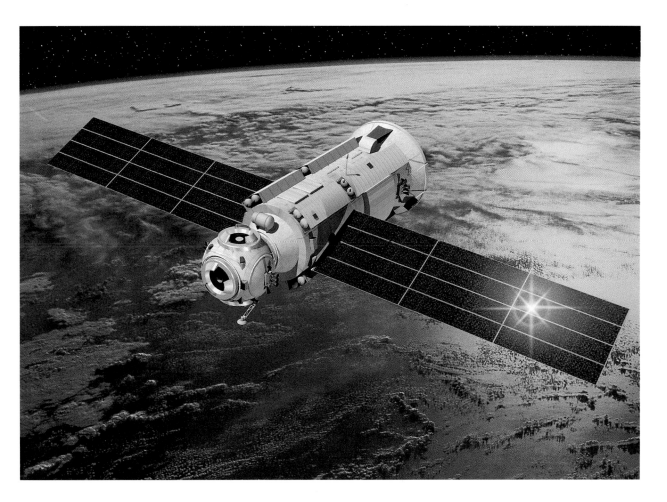

THE RUSSIAN-BUILT "FUNCTIONAL CARGO BLOCK" (FGB) pictured above will be the first element of the ISS sent into orbit around the Earth. This autonomous module has a powerful propulsion and orientation system to adjust its orbit. Large storage tanks ensure that it will not run out of fuel. Two solar arrays will supply electrical power. The Universal Docking Module (UDM) will be attached to the bow of the FGB in 2001. It has connection ports for three more modules and docking ports for Soyuz capsules transporting astronauts and for unmanned Progress capsules transporting supplies.

Russia will build a large part of the ISS. Since these components will equal about 35% of the total station, Russia will be entitled to about one third of the use rights. Russia is building:

What does Russia's contribution include?

- **1 Functional Cargo Block (financed by the USA)**
- **1 pressurized Service Module**
- **2 research laboratories**
- **1 Science and Power Platform (SPP) for external experiments**
- **3 docking nodes**
- **Progress supply vehicles**
- **Soyuz rescue capsules**

Russia retains sole use rights to its own modules. The fixed research equipment installed in these modules does not conform to Western experimental configurations and is not interchangeable with them. Within the overall ISS complex, the Russian components practically form a separate station on the scale of the Mir, with separate energy supply, life support, and research capacities.

Russia will play the most important part during the initial construction of the space station. For the first few years, Russia's modules will form the logistical core of the overall space station complex.

In November 1998, the first element, the "Functional Cargo Block" will be launched from the Baikonur Cosmodrome in Kazakhstan. Like all the Russian space station modules, the FGB resembles the cylindrical Mir elements. It is 13.5 feet in diameter, 41 feet long, and weighs 21 tons. This "control module," which is vital for the station's construction, is a joint contribution; it was commissioned and paid for by the United States.

The FGB is a self-supporting vehicle that will provide power for the other elements during the early phases of assembly. It also has a propulsion system that will adjust the station's orbit, and storage tanks for fuel. Solar array panels on either side of the module will generate about 1 kilowatt of energy. During the construction phase, the FGB will be responsible for keeping the ISS in an orbit about 220 miles above the Earth. In later stages of assembly, the FGB's functions will be assumed by other elements and the FGB will be used primarily for storage.

The Russian Service Module is scheduled to be launched in April 1999. Once in orbit it will dock with the FGB and take over many of its functions. It will also provide a life-support system for the first modules. It has quarters for three astronauts, and from mid-1999 on, a crew will live on the space station and carry out the assembly work. At the rear of the Service Module is a docking adapter for crew and supply capsules.

In the second half of the year 2002, the two Russian research modules, RM1 and RM2, will be sent into orbit and connected to the Service Module.

According to original plans, the International Space Station should have looked like this at the end of 1999, after the first elements had been assembled. The plans were revised in mid 1998 and some of the Russian components will not be mounted until 2001 or later. The Russian FGB and the Service Module (at left), will still be two of the first modules sent into orbit, but the prominent energy tower (SPP) and the Universal Docking Module (UDM) beneath it won't be launched until early 2001. To the right, the American lab module (US LAB) is connected to the Russian modules by Node 1. The central section of the large truss is also in place above US LAB. Below the Russian UDM, a Soyuz capsule has docked.

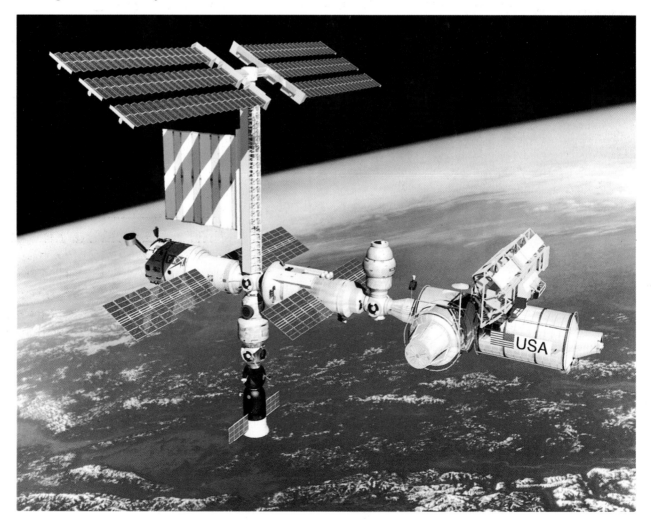

The Japanese astronaut Chiaki Mukai gained space experience on the 1994 Spacelab mission IML-2 (International Microgravity Laboratory) aboard the American Space Shuttle. Dr. Mukai participated in numerous experiments and microgravity studies and investigated the biological effects of space travel on her own body. Through participation in such Spacelab flights, the Japanese space agency NASDA has prepared its scientists for the country's role in the International Space Station.

What is Japan's contribution to the space station?

Japan, too, has been busy in recent years preparing its contributions to the International Space Station. In 1992 the Japanese participated in a joint Spacelab venture, and during this flight, Japanese scientists developed a number of experiments that focused primarily on biomedical and materials studies in microgravity. Several Japanese astronauts have flown on American space missions and have worked on the Russian Mir station performing experiments and studying the effects of shorter and longer space stays on humans.

Japan will provide significant research facilities on the International Space Station. Japan's hardware contribution amounts to a total share of 8%, and consists of the cylindrical Japanese Experiment Module (JEM) and the Experiment Logistics Module (ELM), which includes an external platform and a robotic arm.

The large cylindrical Japanese Experiment Module (JEM) looks much like the American lab modules. It measures 14 feet in diameter and 36 feet in length, and weighs 16 tons empty. In January 2002 it will be transported to the space station by the U. S. Space Shuttle. In addition to the supply systems for life support, power distribution, and communications, it also includes an airlock to permit access to the external platform and a control unit for the platform's robotic arm. Inside the lab module ten double experiment racks will be arranged along the sides of the central aisle. Up to four astronauts can work here on their experiments simultaneously.

Extensive experimental systems and storage space are also housed in the smaller Experiment Logistics Module (ELM). Mounted on top of the large lab cylinder, the ELM is likewise 14 feet 5 inches in diameter but only 12 feet 9 inches high. The astronauts can move between the two modules through a wide hatch.

The Japanese "exposed facility" measures 13 feet 9 inches wide by 16 feet long. On this "balcony," scientists will be able to expose material samples to outer space for extended periods to test the effects of extreme temperature changes and intense cosmic rays on them. The experiments can be manipulated or replaced using the large robotic arm. When astronauts need to examine the experiments directly, they can be moved into and out of the interior of the lab module through an airlock.

The Japanese space station module will be allotted a maximum of 25 kilowatts of electric power from the station's central power supply for short periods. Experimental results can be transmitted to ground control near Tokyo at up to 100 megabytes per second.

Japan is dependent on the other participating countries for the transportation of supplies, since its own H2 booster rockets have only a very limited payload capacity. Like all the partners, however, Japan may offset its costs by leasing part of its extensive laboratory facilities to interested countries, organizations, or research institutions. About half of the Japanese laboratory capacity will be made available to the United States as compensation for its organizational services in building and maintaining the space station.

THE JAPANESE EXPERIMENT MODULE (JEM) is actually quite complex, consisting of four different elements (see picture below). At its center is the cylindrical pressurized cabin. There are two Experiment Logistics Modules (ELM) attached: one on top, the ELM-PS (pressurized section), and one on the outside, the ELM-ES (exposed section), a platform with a robotic arm. In a few years, Japan will thus have considerable laboratory and experimental facilities in orbit. Like their colleagues in other countries, Japanese experts hope that the costly biomedical and materials science experiments in space will some day lead to commercial applications that will recover at least part of the money spent on the station.

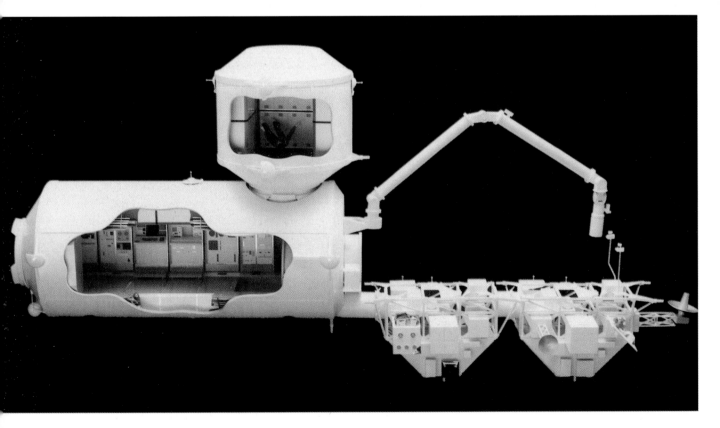

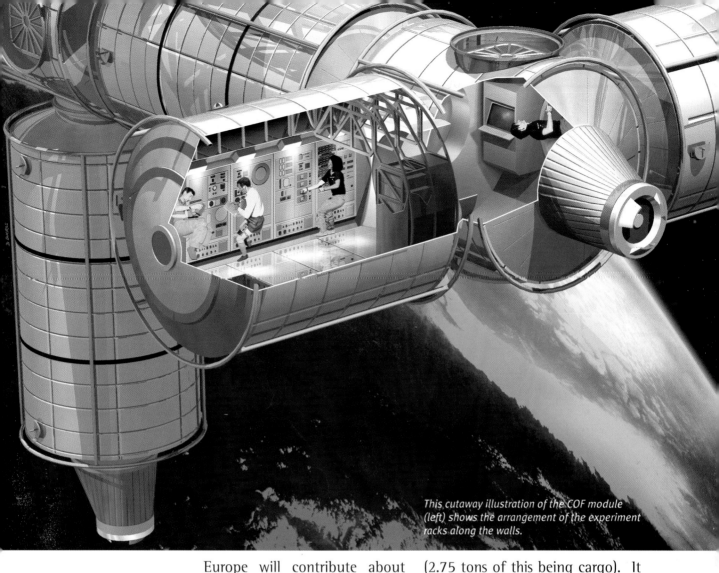

This cutaway illustration of the COF module (left) shows the arrangement of the experiment racks along the walls.

LIKE SPACELAB, the European "Columbus Orbital Facility" (COF) will travel into space aboard the U. S. Space Shuttle. It will dock at Node 2 of the International Space Station complex and will be positioned exactly opposite the Japanese JEM module. Both labs will draw their electricity and other basic utilities from the ISS central supply unit.

> **What will the European module include?**

Europe will contribute about 6% of the construction and operating costs for the ISS. The core of the European contribution will be a laboratory module called the "Columbus Orbital Facility" or COF. The basic design for the COF module and its experiment racks draws on principles developed in Germany some twenty years ago for the European Spacelab project.

The new European Columbus lab will consist of a pressurized cylindrical unit made of aluminum and measuring 21 feet in length and 15 feet in diameter. It will have a launch weight of 13.8 tons (2.75 tons of this being cargo). It will dock at Node 2 of the space station. Although the European module is relatively small compared to the others, it contains ten "International Standard Payload Racks," where scientific instruments and research equipment are installed. To accommodate as many of these racks as possible, designers used every bit of free space. Racks will be mounted on both sides of the central aisle, on the ceiling, and in the space below the floor. When it arrives at the ISS, the COF will be connected to Node 2, which will supply it with water, electricity, and a data transfer system.

The COF module will carry its own environmental monitoring

and control system for recycling cabin air. A water heating and cooling system will maintain an appropriate temperature in the module. There is also a central power system distributing electricity to the various control systems as well as to experiment racks and to other instruments. A data management system will convey experimental data to the station's central communication unit.

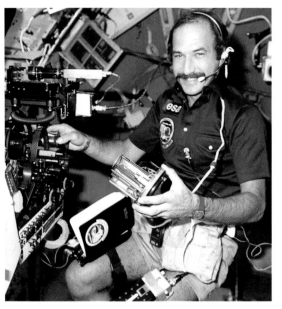

The Dutch astronaut Wubbo Ockels is shown during the 1985 Spacelab mission D-1 aboard Space Shuttle 61-A. He is working with the "Fluid Physics Module" to test the behavior of liquids in microgravity.

The COF module will be permanently connected to the International Space Station. It will be used primarily for experiments in materials science and for research in fundamental physics, fluid physics, biosciences, and medicine.

As an official participant in the International Space Station, Europe can also send astronauts to the space station on a regular basis. Current plans foresee sending two astronauts per year into orbit as ISS crew members, each serving for a period of about two months. They will work on general ISS operations as well as on scientific projects.

All space station activities will be planned and coordinated down to the minutest detail. American, Russian, Japanese and European astronauts will follow a daily rotation as they orbit the Earth.

THE COF MODULE'S EXTERNAL SHELL has a stabilizing criss-cross structure as can be seen in the picture below. The lab module will also be covered with a special foil that will protect it from damage by intensive sunlight, low space temperatures, and dangerous micrometeorites. The module is planned to last for at least 10 years.

What is the Canadian robotic arm like?

Canada has participated in NASA's space projects for many years, and is now supplying the "Mobile Servicing System" (MSS) for the International Space Station. This is a large, flexible robotic arm, which can be used to move massive modules, space station elements, and payloads. Canada's contribution earns it a share in the use of the space station, including occasional missions aboard the orbiting complex for its own astronauts. Canada will assume a 2% share of the space station's maintenance costs.

The MSS will be used to assemble the many components of the station, and to move them again if necessary. Naturally such a tool does not need to lift heavy weights as it would on Earth, since it will be used in zero gravity. Nonetheless, a great deal of electrical pow-

er is required to set a massive resting body in motion, and to stop it again once it is in position. In order to transport large inert masses effectively, the robotic arm must be not only very strong, but also very flexible and extremely precise.

Canada has worked on devices like this for several decades now. Twenty years ago Canada developed a robotic arm for the Space Shuttle. This manipulator was used to load and unload objects from the orbiting Shuttle's cargo bay. Such operations are controlled from the Shuttle cockpit. The Space Shuttle's robotic arm consisted of three segments with joints that have a very wide range of movement. In over 15 years of Shuttle missions it has proved its value as a "crane" and as a platform for astronauts working on difficult extravehicular tasks while in orbit.

The new Mobile Servicing System (MSS) that Canada is now furnishing for the International Space Station consists of three main components. The arm itself – the Space Station Remote Manipulator System (SSRMS) – has a "hand" at one end and is attached to the Mobile Base System (MBS) at the other. The MBS is attached to a system that moves it along tracks on the central truss system to any of the fixed ports. At these anchor ports the Latching End Effector connects it to power supply and control lines. In this way it can be used almost anywhere on the space station. The system also has cameras to monitor the arm at work. These cameras convey information about the progress of the work to the MSS's electronic control system as well as to the astronauts.

Another component of the Canadian Mobile Servicing System is a smaller robot, the "Special-Purpose Dexterous Manipulator"

with two extendible tool arms. The SPDM can be attached to the end of the large robotic arm, and used for especially difficult and detailed work, such as repairs on fuel and coolant lines or replacing material specimens in experiments.

Astronauts can control the Canadian Mobile Servicing System's movements from the space station cockpit, or from outside the space station. The robot's electronics are even able to obey some verbal commands. All an astronaut needs to do is to speak a command, and the machine reacts to the human voice and performs the corresponding action.

Canada will spend some 1.1 billion U. S. dollars by the year 2001 on developing the MSS and other smaller space station components. Most of the cost will be covered by industries, research facilities, and scientific institutions interested in the space station.

THE MOBILE SERVICING SYSTEM (MSS) is Canada's contribution to the International Space Station. This system consists of several parts (see picture below). The Space Station Remote Manipulator System (SSRMS or simply RMS) is the actual robotic arm. The Mobile Transporter (MT) is the movable base attached to the truss assembly that allows the robotic arm to travel along the truss. The SSRMS is connected to the MT by the Mobile Base System (MBS). The SSRMS is scheduled for installation in December of 1999 and will be used in a fixed position at first. The MT and MBS will be delivered in mid 2000, and from then on the robotic arm can be used at other points on the truss assembly.

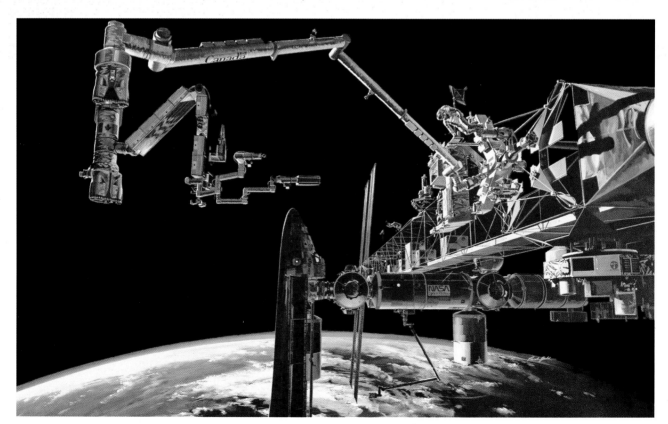

Astronaut Mark C. Lee (right), on the end of
the Remote Manipulator System (RMS) arm,
performs a patch task on the worn insulation
material of the Hubble Space Telescope (HST).
Astronaut Steven L. Smith assists with the
patching.

Life and Work on the Space Station

<table>
<tr><td>

What will an astronaut's life on the station be like?

</td></tr>
</table>

Living conditions aboard the ISS will probably draw on both American and Russian approaches to manned space flight. The Soviet Union – now Russia – gathered a wealth of experience in this field during their record long-term space flights.

A space mission's success starts with the selection of suitable astronaut teams. The men and women participating in the mission will need more than the relevant scientific and linguistic skills; they must be able to get along well with their fellow crewmembers. Working on difficult experiments in a confined space and under conditions of weightlessness can be stressful, and the members of the crew will need to cooperate to accomplish all of their work.

Crewmembers will probably gear their daily routine to the American ground control center in Houston, Texas. This means getting up at about eight o'clock in the morning Central Standard Time, with about eight hours each for work, recreation and sleep. Two astronaut teams working 12-hour shifts will look after special experiments, which will have to be monitored around the clock. This will be done using something like the "red" and "blue" teams on Spacelab missions.

ONE OF THE MOST IMPORTANT EXPERIMENTAL UNITS on board the space station will be the large centrifuge, which is 6 feet in diameter. This instrument will make it possible to expose material samples to varying degrees of gravity for short periods of time.

An engineer operating the centrifuge.

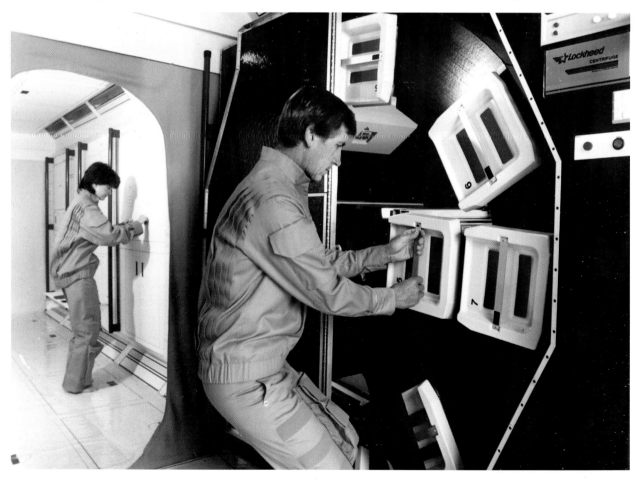

56

Astronauts during an outboard maneuver. The robotic arm is clearly visible.

NUMEROUS SPACE WALKS OR "EVAS" (extravehicular activities) will be necessary for assembling the space station in orbit. They will be physically very demanding for the astronauts. Work outside the station is strenuous and potentially dangerous. Pulse rates quickly rise to 120 or more beats per minute. Automatically or manually controlled robotic arms will assist the astronauts in performing their tasks.

The fixed time schedules for daily planning may shift as the mission goes on. They depend largely on the astronaut crew's state of health as well as on the progress of various experiments and on possible organizational and technical problems. Russian long-term space flights on board Mir developed the following daily pattern: nine hours for sleep and personal hygiene; eight hours of scientific work; two hours in total for three meals; two hours of fitness training; two hours of recreation; one hour of radio contact with ground control.

With the exception of the sleep periods, various activities may always be mixed and the longer working periods will regularly be interrupted by other activities. On board Mir the cosmonauts' experimental and working phase was, for example, curtailed by the fact that they frequently had to deal with defective technical systems in their orbital complex. Similar developments may be envisaged for the International Space Station. Therefore time planning must not be too rigid.

The members of the ISS crew will spend most of their leisure and recreation time in the habitation module (US HAB), which has special sleeping cabins for the crewmembers. This is also where the "portholes" will be situated: facilities for observing the Earth's surface, and equipment for private telephone calls, or even occasional video calls. The cabins will also be fitted with reading lamps and separate air systems, as well as storage space for some personal items. Astronauts can listen to their favorite music on a cassette recorder.

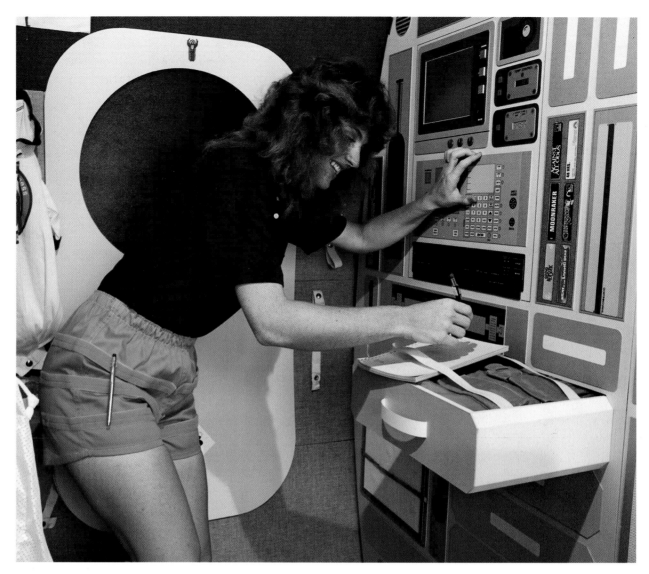

Apart from the sleeping cabins,

<table>
<tr><td>

What will the Habitation Module look like?

</td></tr>
</table>

the habitation module will also contain a bathroom for the astronauts – with a special toilet facility, a wash basin, and a shower. These systems must work perfectly and reliably in microgravity. Without these specially designed fixtures, water would just float around in the cabin after it was used instead of going "down the drain."

The breathing atmosphere on board the space station will correspond to breathing air on Earth:

80 percent nitrogen and 20 percent oxygen. The pressure will be similar to Earth's – about 1 bar. Air on board the space station will, however, be much cleaner than on Earth. People suffering from hay fever will find no irritants in orbit. The temperature can be adjusted to levels between 60 and 90 degrees Fahrenheit.

Interior designers and psychologists specializing in the effects of color are co-operating on the space station's interior design in order to create an environment that is as pleasant as possible for the astronauts during their months in orbit. Nevertheless, the ISS as-

DURING THE PRE-LAUNCH PERIOD NASA is testing many options for the interior furnishings of their research and habitation modules. Whatever style they choose, it must meet the technical and scientific requirements for the installation of the experiment racks. Designers are trying to make the modules as comfortable as possible so that astronauts will have good working conditions while carrying their experiments. One of NASA's interior decorators (above) takes a close look at personal storage space in a crew cabin.

tronauts will feel as if they were on board a large submarine with many corridors branching off — there will be only very few windows or view points.

The floor surfaces for all modules will be given a darker color in order to emphasize the "floor feeling." The walls with the experiment racks and the ceilings will be painted in lighter colors — similar to room ceilings on Earth. The dining and kitchen areas as well as the individual sleeping cabins will be furnished to make astronauts feel "at home."

Whenever possible, the men and women on the space station will eat their meals together in the American habitation module. Crewmembers must fasten their seat belts during mealtimes so as not to float away during dinner. Russian long-term missions have shown that six astronauts will need about 20 tons of supplies per year — about one Shuttle load.

The astronauts must take particular care when eating soups or drinking liquids. These substances have to be sucked through a straw from a closed container. Any droplets of water, coffee or juice which have accidentally escaped must immediately be cleaned up before they can find their way into the technical systems where they could cause a short-circuit.

When they are launched, space station modules will contain dehydrated food supplies. These are mainly ready-made meals, which the astronauts have to prepare in the microwave, using cold or hot water. Apart from three pre-cooked meals, there will be a lot of frozen food on board the space station, and also snacks to eat in between meals.

Crewmembers will take turns preparing the food — a practice tested in earlier space flights. The astronaut on "kitchen duty" will need about half an hour to prepare a meal for six people. Clearing up after the meal will take roughly the same time.

Pilot Terence T. Henricks "rows" on the modified treadmill device used by crewmembers for biomedical tests and for exercising. Earlier, they found that the treadmill would not support subjects in "running" mode. In the background, Mission Specialist Mario Runco Jr. waits for his turn on the treadmill.

The American, Japanese, and European lab modules have all been designed to accommodate a variety of new research projects

How will the experiment racks be used?

during the years that they will spend in orbit. Based on experience gained during Spacelab missions, the ISS partners have developed a special payload system that makes it easy to share the same facilities. Experiments or "payloads" will be held in "racks" known as "International Standard Payload Racks" (ISPR). The racks themselves can be installed or removed easily, and so can the experiments in them. All of the Western partners will make their experiment racks with the same dimensions and power connections. These racks can be easily connected to the interfaces in the different lab modules. The usual arrangement

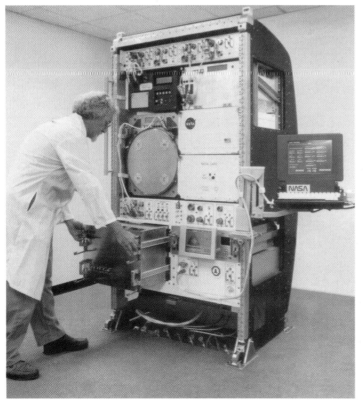

will probably be racks on both sides of a central aisle.

International Standard Payload Racks are 41.6 inches wide, 80 inches high and roughly 40 inches deep with a slightly curved back to fit the cylinder wall. Their payload capacity is 56 cubic feet, which corresponds to about 1,540 pounds in weight. The payload racks used in the American, Japanese and European lab modules are water-cooled and maintain an operating temperature of between 60 and 68 degrees Fahrenheit for the instruments that are inserted into them. Some of the racks are also designed so that they can freeze or heat the experiments they contain — "shock freezing" to temperatures as low as minus 94° F and heating to temperatures as high as 2,732° F. In addition, the racks can produce vacuum conditions. They are designed for a maximum power intake of 20 kilowatts.

The Americans, Japanese, and Europeans have agreed on standard measurements for these payload racks so that all elements are interchangeable and any experiment can be installed anywhere in the Western part of the space station. The Russian lab modules have their own unique design — one not compatible with Western racks.

According to the lab use plan agreed on between the various International Space

EXPRESS RACKS (short for EXpedite the PRocessing of Experiments to Space Station) are specially constructed rack systems for smaller, short-term experiments. Such experiments can easily be inserted into the EXPRESS racks and then — with equal ease — taken out and brought back to Earth.

IN COOPERATION WITH LABS ON EARTH, the ISS will carry out a thorough inventory of materials and processes to see which ones are most likely to benefit from experiments and testing in microgravity. In addition, scientists are planning long-term experiments that will last several months and will examine the basic laws of nature more closely. Such experiments may even lead to the discovery of new fundamental principles of physics and chemistry.

At left, a model of a double rack for the space station.

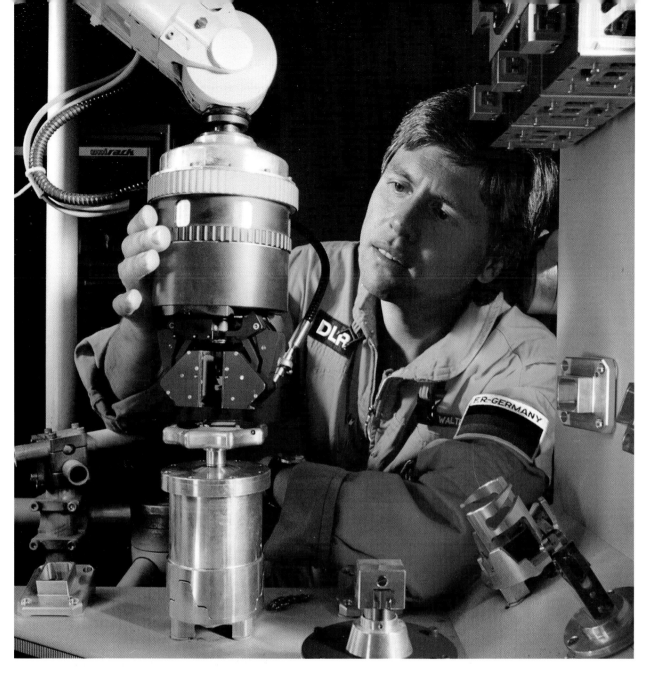

ROBOTIC INSTRUMENTS will often assist astronauts in lengthy and tedious experiments. Once they are appropriately programmed, such robots can agitate or substitute test materials at regular intervals. Such robotic arms have joints that allow them to move into almost any position. They also have a grasping finger that can insert samples into holders and then remove them again.

Station partners, the United States will control a major share of the experimental space in the Western modules of the ISS. Since NASA is providing the basic framework to which the other Western partners will attach their modules, the United States will even control a share of the research space contributed by other Western partners — 20% of the overall research capacity of the European and Japanese modules. For example, in the European Space Agency's (ESA) COF module, five of the ten racks will be allocated to researchers from the member nations of the ESA. Of the remaining five racks reserved for other ISS partners, NASA will control two. As a result, there will be an international mix of scientists working side-by-side in the various laboratories, and not just scientists from the sponsoring nation.

This international working environment will be one of the important contributions of the ISS, helping to foster global understanding and cooperation.

Will there be hotels in space?

In the last decade, manned space flight has made astonishing progress. The International Space Station now being assembled in orbit is the most ambitious manned project so far. Scientists will live and work on board the ISS for several months at a time. As facilities for long-term space stays improve, the question arises whether or not ordinary human beings might be able to travel into space in the near future — as tourists spending their vacation on a space station rather than in New York or Hawaii. After all, a hundred years ago few people dreamed it might be possible one day to travel by air to any destination on Earth in just a few hours. Nowadays, air travel has become quite normal. Why shouldn't vacations in space become just as normal?

During an International Symposium on Space Tourism in Bremen, Germany, more than 100 experts recently discussed this very topic. Many of the participants believe that space tourism might be possible in the not too distant future. At present, space flight is far too expensive for tourist use, but this will surely change in the future. Some experts predict that it will probably be about 30 years — a conservative estimate, they say — before the first tourist flights into space can begin.

Designers also presented a model for a possible space hotel at the congress. It consisted of a number of residential units spinning around a fixed center. The spinning was supposed to produce at least a limited gravity, thus reducing or eliminating altogether the risk of space sickness for hotel guests. This aspect of the space hotel was probably taken from Wernher von Braun's plans for a space station.

An artist's depiction of a ring-shaped space hotel. It would spin around a central axis, thus creating a minimum gravity.

That is what a passenger spacecraft might look like. At right is a model of the X-34 reusable space transporter now being developed by NASA.

Some experts on tourism suggest that by the year 2025 there might be as many as 20 million space tourists. If the number of people interested in space vacations is indeed this high, it might help solve the most pressing problem: exorbitant transport costs. For one astronaut to travel to the Mir station and stay on board costs well over 20 million dollars. No "normal wage earner" could afford that price! If transport rockets were used to capacity, however, and flew frequently, the costs might go down quite quickly.

Transportation costs aren't the only obstacle, however. Tourists looking for a "vacation" in space will surely be concerned with comfort. Not many people are likely to spend a good part of their vacation cramped in a small space capsule, as astronauts today must do. The passenger space vehicle would probably be a one-stage, multi-use vehicle. It would have to have a larger, much more comfortable cabin capable of accommodating 50 to 100 passengers. There are already plans for such transport vehicles. Designers frequently present new models, particularly in the United States. The models are usually based on the Venture Star. A space hotel would, of course, have to be more comfortable and more luxurious than the ISS.

For the time being, technology is not yet up to these challenges. Before any of this can be possible, we need to make major advances in propulsion technology and materials science. As a result, we can't say for sure when the first tourist flights into space will take place. It could easily take much longer than tourism experts predict for all of this to become a reality — but some day it will surely be possible to spend your vacation in orbit and see the Earth from space!

List of Acronyms

ASTP	Apollo Soyuz Test Project		MT	Mobile Transporter
ATV	Automatic Transport Vehicle		MSS	Mobile Servicing System
COF	Columbus Orbital Facility		NASA	National Aeronautics and Space Administration
CRV	Crew Return Vehicle			
ELM	Experiment Logistics Module		NASDA	Japanese Space Agency
ESA	European Space Agency		POIC	Payload Operations and Integrations Center
EVA	extravehicular activity			
FGB	Functionalui Germaticheskii Blok: Functional Cargo Block		RM	Research Module
			RMS	Remote Manipulator System
ISPR	International Standard Payload Rack		SM	Service Module
ISS	International Space Station		SPDM	Special Purpose Dexterous Manipulator
ITA	Integrated Truss Assembly		SPP	Science and Power Platform
JEM	Japanese Experiment Module		SS-CC	Space Station Command Center
LSM	Life Support Module		SSRMS	Space Station Remote Manipulator System
MBS	Mobile Base System			
			UDM	Universal Docking Module
			US HAB	United States Habitation Module
			US LAB	United States Laboratory
			USML	U.S. Microgravity Laboratory

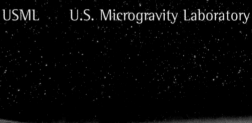